Vegetarian Keto Diet for Beginners

How to Live the Keto Lifestyle as a Healthy Vegetarian

by

Dr. Marie Taketo

Why You Should Read This Book

Congratulations on taking your first step towards a healthy lifestyle as a "ketotarian". This journey that you are on is going to be exciting and empowering. If you study this book and follow the simple step-by-step meal plan described in the subsequent chapters, you are going to lose no less than 5 kgs (11 pounds) within 2 weeks. Hundreds if not thousands of people like you have done this before. Something as effective as the keto diet becomes famous only because it gives clearly noticeable results.

This book in particular, has been designed to give you a concise understanding of what a ketogenic diet is, what the rules and goals are, how to follow it as a vegetarian. From understanding the definition of ketosis to preparing delicious keto-friendly breakfast foods, we are going to cover the whole nine yards. Now, let's get chopping!

Table of Contents

Chapter 1:

Ketogenic Diet – The Basics

In this chapter, we will discuss the basics behind the ketogenic diet. What is it? How does it work? What is ketosis? How do I get into ketosis, and what do I do once I'm there?

What is the ketogenic diet?

The ketogenic diet is an eating style that focuses on high fat and low carbohydrate intake. Protein intake in the ketogenic diet is about the same as recommended for all healthy people. You may hear the ketogenic diet referred to as a low-carbohydrate diet, high-fat, modified Atkins, or simply "keto". The word "ketogenic" means "ketone-producing", which is the aim of the ketogenic diet.

Although there are several different types of the ketogenic diet, typically people aim for macronutrient ratios (macros) of 75% of calories from fat, 20% from protein, and 5 to 10% from carbohydrates. We'll get into macros later in this chapter, so don't worry about those too much right now.

How does the ketogenic diet work?

You've probably heard about the ketogenic diet, but most people don't actually understand the science behind the diet and how it works. Without trying to turn this into a chemistry course, we'll provide a quick overview of the science involved in the ketogenic diet.

The human body is trained to depend on glucose to provide energy for its organs and tissues. When you consume the Standard American Diet (or any eating pattern that is high in carbohydrates), glucose is present in abundant quantities, and the body can use glucose for energy or store it for later as **glycogen** in the liver and muscles.

In the ketogenic diet, however, a metabolic state known as **ketosis** is sought. In ketosis, the body no longer has a large amount of carbohydrates (glucose) available to break down for energy, and as a result, fat stored in our body is broken down to **ketones** which then circulate in the blood to distribute energy. This happens when the body breaks down stored fat to triglycerides, a process that releases ketones as a byproduct. Chemically, ketones are acids, and they are removed from the body in urine.

However, the body still requires *some* glucose to function – this is why we cannot consume a zero-carbohydrate diet on keto! Some organs, including the brain, require glucose in order to function. While the brain can directly use glucose, it cannot directly get energy from fat, which is why ketones are so important in the ketogenic diet. Once you enter ketosis, the liver is responsible for providing glucose to the brain by breaking down stored glycogen. When the liver has exhausted all glycogen supplies, it starts breaking down fatty acids from your diet (which is why we consume such high quantities of fat in the ketogenic diet) and body fat (which is why you can lose weight so rapidly on keto). Pretty fascinating, right? It is believed that ketosis developed as a human adaptation to starvation.

What are the requirements?

As promised, it's time for a primer on macros (macronutrients). If you know anyone who's big into weight lifting or bodybuilding, chances are that you've heard them talk at length about their macros. So, it's time to let you in on their secret! Macros refer to the 3 major nutrients our body needs to function – fat, protein, and carbohydrates. Each serves a different role, so we have different needs for each. Also, different people have varied needs depending on how much they weigh, what they do for exercise, and other factors like chronic diseases. So, first we break our diet down into the 3 nutrient categories. Carbohydrates and protein have 4 calories per gram, while fat has 9 per gram. If you divide your total caloric intake up accordingly, you can figure out what percentage of your diet is from each macronutrient. Let's not stress too much over math here, but here's an example:

- You eat 2000 calories a day.
- You choose to have 10% of your daily calories from carbohydrates.
- 2000 calories x 0.1 = 200 calories.
- 200 calories / 4 calories per gram = 50 grams of carbohydrates allowed.

That was easy, right? We just determined that, in order to limit your carbohydrate intake to 10% of your calories, you can consume 50 grams (or 200 calories) of carbohydrates each day. There are a lot more complicated ways to use macros, but you won't really need to worry about that on the ketogenic diet. Just stick to your carbohydrate goal.

Now – we just learned that it's easy to find your macros – so here comes a bit of a curve ball: **NET CARBS**. These are incredibly important when it comes to the ketogenic diet, and understanding how to use them can help you add a lot more variety to your meals. Don't worry, calculating net carbs is also super simple!

When you look at a nutrition label, you'll see "Total Carbohydrates" – and that's exactly what it sounds like, the total grams of carbohydrates in 1 serving of the food. This accounts for both sugars and dietary fiber. Pro tip: dietary fiber is your friend on keto! It can be tough to get a lot of fiber since you're limiting fruits, vegetables, and grains – but you should still aim to get a decent amount of fiber each day if possible (maybe 15-25 grams).

Anyway, here's all you need to do: take the number of grams of total carbohydrates and subtract the number of grams of dietary fiber. Boom! There's your net carb number.

A quick example: You check out the package and it has 20 grams of total carbohydrates per serving and 5 grams of dietary fiber. A quick calculation tells you to count this as 15 grams net carbs.

$20\,g - 5\,g = 15\,g$ net carbs

When you set your carbohydrate goal for the day (most people aim for 40-50 grams maximum, but other stricter keto'ers limit theirs to 20 grams) – you will use net carbs.

How can we achieve it?

Typically, it takes approximately 2 to 4 days of very low carbohydrate intake (20-50 grams daily) for your body to enter ketosis. However, ketosis needs can vary for different people based on many factors. It may take longer to enter ketosis (even as long as a few weeks) depending on your carbohydrate intake prior to starting the ketogenic diet, and some people may need to consume less than 20 grams of carbohydrates per day in order to start and maintain ketosis. You can expect to consume about 5 to 10% of your daily calories from carbohydrates – which sounds like more than it is!

We learned A LOT in this chapter! You should now be familiar with the basics of the ketogenic diet, how it works, what macros and net carbs are and how to calculate them, and how to get your body into ketosis. Ready for more? Let's go!

Chapter 2:

Benefits of the Ketogenic Diet

In this chapter, we'll discuss the beneficial effects of the ketogenic diet. These benefits include weight loss, of course – but also many health-related and other positive side effects. It's entirely likely that there are several benefits of the ketogenic diet listed here that you hadn't even considered!

Weight loss

Although a high-fat diet is often blamed for weight gain and obesity, this is only true in the case of a high-fat, high-calorie diet. When done properly, a calorie-controlled ketogenic diet can provide quick, relatively easy, effective weight loss in overweight and obese individuals.

One 2008 study of obese men concluded that after only 4 weeks on the ketogenic diet, each man lost an average of 12 pounds. These men also reported feeling less hungry while following the ketogenic diet. Other studies have shown that low-carbohydrate diets can produce up to 2-3 times more weight loss than low-fat diets.

On that note, the ketogenic diet is also noteworthy for its tendency to decrease hunger. As a result, you'll most likely consume fewer calories, further accelerating weight loss. The ketogenic diet also tends to allow for a greater amount of "water weight" - a result of excess sodium in the kidneys being flushed out due to decreased insulin levels. As an added bonus - the hunger associated with restrictive "diets" is not present.

Health benefits

High-carbohydrate and high-sugar diets can create an environment that fast-tracks the aging process. Diets high in simple carbohydrates may also promote the development of chronic diseases such as type 2 diabetes, some cancers, and cardiovascular diseases, regardless of any preexisting risk factors. It appears that this phenomenon may be due to the inverse relationship between sugar intake and vitamin E (an antioxidant) levels in the body. Decreased levels of antioxidants in the body have been shown to allow for the development of many diseases.

Meanwhile, the ketogenic diet can actually decrease your chances of developing heart disease. Even a short-term ketogenic diet has the ability to improve high cholesterol — both by increasing levels of beneficial HDL and decreasing elevated LDL levels. When the ketogenic diet is followed properly, heart health typically improves.

High-fat diets such as keto have also been linked to a decreased risk of developing breast cancer. Studies are also assessing whether or not the ketogenic diet used simultaneously with chemotherapy and radiation for cancer treatment. It is believed that a high-fat diet could be extremely beneficial due to its effects on oxidative stress and insulin levels, which can both play a part in cancer development.

Low-carbohydrate diets even have the capability to decrease levels of visceral fat in the abdomen – this fat surrounds your organs. This fat is not only uncomfortable and generally regarded as unattractive, but it also carries major health risks when visceral fat levels become excessive. Too much visceral fat can lead to insulin resistance (which can often progress to diabetes), increased systemic inflammation, and metabolic problems. This is great news – not only can you lose a significant amount of weight on the ketogenic diet, but you will likely lose more visceral abdominal fat than on other diets, decreasing your risk for diabetes and heart disease.

If you suffer from high triglycerides (or even if you don't but would rather not develop this problem), the ketogenic diet can also help you. High-carbohydrate diets typically *increase* your triglycerides, a process believed to be attributed to fructose intake.

Hypertension (high blood pressure) can also be resolved by adopting the ketogenic diet. By avoiding long-term hypertension, you can also avoid complications such as kidney disease, stroke, and heart disease.

Have you heard of metabolic syndrome? It's not necessarily a disease, but rather a collection of symptoms that include obesity (specifically in the abdominal area), low HDL cholesterol, elevated triglycerides, insulin resistance, and hypertension. The ketogenic diet has the ability to improve all of these problems, and is being recommended for individuals who already have metabolic syndrome in order to improve their health.

It is also suggested that the ketogenic diet may be beneficial for prevention or reversal of osteoporosis, a bone disorder that often leads to fractures. Osteoporosis occurs frequently in people (especially women) following a low-fat diet, as these diets are not only low in calcium, but also tend to lead to less calcium absorption.

The ketogenic diet can also be beneficial for people with type 2 diabetes or insulin resistance (often referred to as "pre-diabetes"). Not only does this diet work by limiting carbohydrate intake, it also allows your body to require less insulin, which essentially has the ability to clear up insulin resistance as a result.

For women with polycystic ovarian syndrome (PCOS), the ketogenic diet may help them to lose weight, maintain appropriate insulin levels, and improve indicators (blood tests) specifically related to their PCOS – suggesting improvement of the disease.

The ketogenic diet also has the potential to provide benefits related to mental health. More research is still needed, but the ketogenic diet has been proposed as a possible treatment for bipolar disorder. It is suggested that increased metabolic activity in the brain related to protein metabolism could help treat depression and mania triggered by this disorder.

The ketogenic diet has huge implications for improved brain health. First, it has shown to improve cognition in children and tended to make them more alert. The ketogenic diet is often used successfully for people in treatment for brain cancer. Research is also underway to determine if the ketogenic diet can prevent or treat brain injuries or disorders such as Parkinson's disease, Lou Gehrig's disease, autism, multiple sclerosis, and Alzheimer's disease. It has also been suggested that the ketogenic diet could be used to treat some cases of insomnia or other sleep disorders.

Other benefits

The ketogenic diet can even help clear up stubborn acne. Some people may have breakouts that are due to increased blood sugar, which are triggered by a high-carbohydrate diet. By following the ketogenic diet, blood sugar fluctuations are less common and acne may improve.

In this chapter, we learned LOTS of positive changes associated with adopting the ketogenic diet – from weight loss to improved health to so much more!

Chapter 3:

Keto - It's Not For Everyone

This chapter title says it all, right? Every diet has its critics, and no one diet is right for everyone. In this chapter, we'll discuss whether or not the ketogenic diet might be a good fit for you. There are many more aspects to consider than you might have realized. If you have any medical problems, pay close attention here.

As soon as you considered starting the ketogenic diet, you probably started hearing from the critics everywhere – family, friends, coworkers, etc. The ketogenic diet certainly isn't for everyone – and everyone is entitled to their opinion! However, if you've made it this far and done your research, the ketogenic diet is probably a good fit for you.

Who is the ketogenic diet ideal for?

The ketogenic diet is appropriate for most healthy individuals who are looking to lose weight. However, if you have heart disease or diabetes, you should discuss this with your doctor prior to beginning.

The ketogenic diet is also appropriate for many people with type 2 diabetes that is under control. Although circulating levels of glucose are much lower, the blood is able to maintain its glucose levels by breaking down amino acids (from protein) and fatty acids to create glucose.

The ketogenic diet was initially developed as a treatment for children with severe epilepsy (a seizure disorder) that did not respond to other types of treatment. If you suffer from seizures or other types of neurological disorders, the ketogenic diet may also help you experience fewer symptoms! For many people, the ketogenic diet provides better control then anticonvulsant medications, without the side effects.

Who should NOT follow the keto diet?

The ketogenic diet is typically *not* appropriate for children or adolescents. Therefore, if you live with children, you may want to consider whether you are willing to prepare meals for two completely different diets every day.

If you have kidney disease, the ketogenic diet is not for you. Protein intake typically needs to be limited in kidney disease, and the slightly higher level of protein required in the ketogenic diet may worsen the disease. Similarly, people with gout should not follow the ketogenic diet, as it can trigger painful symptoms.

It's also not recommended for pregnant women to follow the ketogenic diet, but it is typically fine during breastfeeding (ask your doctor first, of course!).

Due to the potential for developing diabetic ketoacidosis (a serious, potentially life-threatening complication), the ketogenic diet is not recommended for anyone with type 1 diabetes.

In order to follow the ketogenic diet, you need to be motivated and committed to the lifestyle change. This diet is very strict, and there is no room for "cheat days" or even "cheat meals", as just one high-carbohydrate meal can knock you right out of ketosis and ruin all of your hard work. You need to be willing to try new recipes and cooking styles, and spend a bit of time reading labels in the grocery store and preparing meals in the kitchen. If you are very busy, tend to be unmotivated and give up on diets after a few days or weeks, or if you have a lot of children or other family members to cook for, the ketogenic diet may not be the best fit for your lifestyle.

In this chapter, we took a good hard look at whether the ketogenic diet is right for you. It's appropriate for most people, but of course we don't want anyone to get seriously ill, so make sure you have addressed any health concerns prior to starting.

Chapter 4:

The Vegetarian Keto Diet

Sure, you might have heard of the ketogenic diet – but as a vegetarian, did you ever think that you'd be following a diet that consists of butter, bacon, and meat? In this chapter, we'll discuss how to go keto and maintain your vegetarian lifestyle without losing your mind. Different types of keto-friendly foods and vegetarian sources of protein will be suggested as well. We will also discuss what NOT to eat in order to be as successful as possible on the ketogenic diet.

How to follow keto as a vegetarian

You've most likely seen the depiction of the stereotypical ketogenic diet: meat, butter, and eggs. Of course, these foods certainly have a part in the ketogenic diet, but you're probably wondering how a vegetarian can meet the requirements of the ketogenic diet without meat products. Luckily, you're not strictly limited to those food choices!

For our meat-eating friends, the ketogenic diet is a bit simpler. Meat is typically very low in carbohydrates and high in fat and protein – perfect for keto macros! However, as plant-based folks, vegetarian keto dieters need to be slightly more creative in their meal planning. So where do we start?

What to eat

On the ketogenic diet, you need to consume nearly all of your calories from fat and protein. Vegetarian foods that are commonly used in the ketogenic diet include eggs, cheese, butter, seeds, oils, nuts, and non-starchy vegetables.

People on the ketogenic diet often completely forego vegetable intake – as these can contribute a significant amount of carbohydrates to the diet. While this is useful in theory, you could be missing out on beneficial vitamins, minerals, and antioxidants.

Some of the most popular vegetables that can be consumed on the ketogenic diet include:

- Artichokes
- Asparagus
- Baby corn
- Broccoli
- Brussels sprouts
- Eggplant
- Green beans
- Okra
- Onions
- Salad greens
- Tomatoes
- Turnips
- Water chestnuts.

Certain types of fats are more useful on a ketogenic diet than others. Fats that are recommended include any kind of oil (such as olive or coconut), butter, mayonnaise, and heavy cream. Other types or sources of oils that may be useful while on the ketogenic diet include:

- Almond oil
- Flaxseed oil
- Pumpkin seeds
- Walnuts.

High-fat foods that are also low- or zero-carbohydrate are encouraged on a vegetarian ketogenic diet, including coconut oil, grass-fed butter, whole milk, and full-fat dairy foods.

What not to eat

Obviously, if you've gotten this far, you already know that high-carbohydrate foods are off-limits on the ketogenic diet. This means no conventional bread, pasta, and other carbohydrate-rich treats. This can be difficult to deal with when you first begin the ketogenic diet. However, there are plenty of delicious low-carb versions available for purchase, and many keto-friendly recipes online (as well as later in this book!).

When you first start the ketogenic diet, it can be tempting to choose foods that may have been "off-limits" on other diets, such as processed foods that are high in protein and contain low-quality fats and high levels of sodium (salt). There is certainly room for these foods in the ketogenic diet, but you should not base the majority of your diet around foods that can stall your weight loss.

Although high fat intake is encouraged in the ketogenic diet, it is recommended that trans fat intake be eliminated or restricted as much as possible. Trans fats are often added to processed products to improve their shelf life. These fats can cause a surge in inflammation in the body, as well as increasing cholesterol levels.

Typically, foods eliminated or restricted heavily from the diet include legumes (beans and peas) and other starchy vegetables, fruit, grains, and carbohydrate-heavy sweets and snack foods.

Although fruit cannot usually be consumed on a ketogenic diet, avocado (technically a fruit!) is used frequently since it is high in fat. Some people may also choose to consume blackberries, as they are high in fiber.

How to get enough protein

As we noted earlier, you can't exactly turn to a big chunk of meat to get your protein. As a vegetarian who is also adopting a low-carbohydrate lifestyle, you'll need to focus much more on your vegetarian protein sources such as nuts, seeds, eggs, cheese, and tofu. If you like, you can also add in protein powder and other supplements.

Make sure to keep track of your protein intake when you first start on the ketogenic diet so that you know you are getting enough. The average healthy person requires a minimum of 0.8 grams per kilogram (about 0.36 grams per pound) protein per day, although people on the ketogenic diet typically consume a bit more than that.

Tips for beginners

If you don't care for bland food and previously relied on sugary marinades and dressings to flavor your food, consider adding herbs and spices when you cook. We recommend adding several to your pantry, including basil, cayenne pepper, salt, pepper, cilantro, and chili powder. If you choose to purchase packaged spices, make sure they are no-sugar-added, as many can have hidden sugar included.

If you were a heavy soda drinker prior to the ketogenic diet, you may enjoy drinking unsweetened teas and coffees. Similarly, you may need to swap out the condiments in your refrigerator once you begin the ketogenic diet. There are ketogenic-approved versions of hot sauce, ketchup, mustard, Worcestershire sauce, and salad dressings – again, check the label to confirm that they are no-sugar-added so you can comply with keto as well as possible.

*In this chapter, we learned what **to** eat and what **not to** eat on a vegetarian ketogenic diet. We also discussed some options for vegetarian protein sources, good choices for non-starchy vegetables, and keto-friendly fats and oils.*

Chapter 5:

What to Expect on Keto

Just like every diet, the first few days or weeks on the ketogenic diet can be confusing, difficult, and you may even feel ill. In this chapter, we'll run through what to expect and how to handle it.

Side effects and the "keto flu"

Although it is a fantastic diet that can help you lose weight quickly and easily, the ketogenic diet can also have some unpleasant side effects. However, most of these symptoms are typically minor and short-term after first beginning the ketogenic diet.

The "keto flu" is a combination of symptoms such as fatigue, vomiting, and nausea that can occur shortly after beginning the ketogenic diet. These problems typically resolve within a week of starting the ketogenic diet, and many people feel very energetic and their mood is much more positive than usual once the symptoms are gone.

Insomnia and changes to your sleep are also possible when transitioning to the ketogenic diet. This may continue for as long as a few weeks, but long-term ketogenic diet users typically report that keto actually improves their sleep overall.

Digestive issues may occur when you first begin the ketogenic diet – diarrhea and/or constipation are common. However, these are typically short-term problems due simply to a drastic change in diet, and they tend to resolve quickly.

Some people experience changes to the smell of their breath while on the ketogenic diet. This occurs because one of the types of ketones (acetate) is breathed out rather than removed in the urine. Your breath may smell fruity or a bit like nail polish remover (which also contains acetone!). However, it is typically not too overwhelming, and you can keep sugar-free mints and gums around if you are concerned about bad breath. Make sure to check the labels to make sure these do not have any carbohydrates in them.

How can you deal with the keto flu? Try to get extra electrolytes in when you are feeling poorly – but make sure you are not consuming hidden sugar or carbohydrates.

How your body changes on keto

As with any change in diet, there is a potential for vitamin and mineral deficiencies. The ketogenic diet has the added potential for this because low carbohydrate intake often results in taking in fewer nutrients. When you start the ketogenic diet, make it a point to let your doctor and/or dietitian know so that they can keep an eye on your bloodwork and watch for any possible nutritional problems.

Common supplements for people on the ketogenic diet include vitamin D, calcium, selenium, and B vitamins. Others may include folic acid and iron, especially in women. Make sure that any supplements you choose to take are sugar-free and carbohydrate-free and ask the pharmacist to provide a pill form rather than liquid.

There are a few health-related side effects that can occur due to the ketogenic diet, but they are fairly rare. These problems include kidney stones, muscle breakdown, and acidosis (this lowers the pH of your blood). To avoid serious complications, simply pay attention to your body, and if something doesn't feel right, have your doctor check it out.

In this chapter, we learned about a few changes to expect when you start the ketogenic diet. By knowing what might occur and preparing ahead of time, you can save yourself some trouble when the time comes!

Chapter 6:

Keto Tools & Resources

In this chapter, we'll simply provide a few resources and tools that might be helpful to you as you start your journey into a ketogenic lifestyle. As you progress, you'll likely find other options that you like, but these are just a few that are helpful for beginners.

- **Atkins Net Carb Counter** – This document has a ton of information about the net carb content of a variety of different foods. If you're not the type of person who likes to use an app for that and you'd rather have a printout, this is for you!

- **Keto Apps** – There are SO MANY out there, but here are a few of our favorites:
  - **MyFitnessPal** – Not keto-specific of course, but you can easily plan meals and track your macros just like you would on any other type of diet.
  - **KetoDietApp** – Food and macro tracking.
  - **Total Keto Diet** – LOTS of delicious keto-friendly recipes, as well as a keto macro calculator.
  - **Carb Manager** – Macro counter, diet tracker, and 1 million + foods!
  - **Senza** – Net carb barcode scanner and tracker.
  - **8Fit** – Includes workouts and tracking.

- **Macro Calculators** – There are hundreds out there, and they'll all pretty much give you the same information. If you're not the kind of person who wants to calculate your macros by hand, try finding a macro calculator that you like and bookmarking it!

Chapter 7:

Keto Tips & Tricks

In this chapter, we'll discuss a few different tricks of the keto trade that can help you maximize your results and minimize your effort. Not all of these tips may work for you, so choose carefully!

Intermittent fasting

After you've been on the ketogenic diet for a little while and have gotten the hang of it, intermittent fasting (IF) may be something worth trying. We don't recommend starting IF until you've been keto for at least a few months, because it does take your body time to adjust.

Contrary to how its name might sound, you're not actually going to be starving yourself on IF. Rather, it just means changing the timing of your meals a bit.

There are a few different types of IF, and you may want to try more than one before deciding which is best for you. We'll only discuss 2 types here, since things can get pretty complicated.

16/8 intermittent fasting splits up your day into 2 different sections – a 16-hour period (including overnight) where you fast (water and tea are fine) and then an 8-hour period during which you eat all of your meals. For example, you might fast from 6pm until 10am, then consume all of your meals for the day between 10am and 6pm.

Simply **skipping a meal** is also a form of IF. Many people will choose to skip breakfast, which essentially has the same effect as 16/8 IF, in which you're going a prolonged period without food.

Exercise

Just like with any other diet, you'll get better results if you combine keto with exercise. You don't need to do anything specific – whatever type of exercise you enjoy is just fine. Try to be active for at least 30 minutes per day on most (5 or 6) days of the week. If you have joint pain or any medical problems, make sure to discuss exercise with your doctor before starting something new.

During the first few weeks of the ketogenic diet, you may not feel like exercising due to the "keto flu" or other symptoms. Don't push yourself beyond your limits, just try to get some light exercise in when you are feeling fine, and work up from there.

Supplements

There are many supplements out there that claim to be important for the keto diet – how do you know what's true and what's not worth the money? Here are a few tried and true supplements that can be a worthwhile addition.

MCT oil is oil made from medium-chain triglycerides (hence the name!), usually from coconut oil. MCT oil is digested more easily than other fats and oils, and many people on keto like to add it to things like salad dressing, bulletproof coffee, and smoothies. MCT oil can help promote weight loss due to its effects on the hormones leptin and peptide YY – which help you feel full. It can also be used for energy by the brain, and the liver can convert MCT oil to ketones. If you choose to add MCT oil to your supplement regimen, limit it to about 1 to 2 tbsp per day and make sure you are replacing another fat or oil in your diet, rather than just adding it.

Protein powder can be another great addition to your diet. There are many different types out there (whey, egg white, pea, hemp, and many more), so you'll have to decide what works best for you. In general, look for a carbohydrate-free or low-carbohydrate formula. Some people choose to use collagen powder instead, which is 100% protein and contains no carbohydrates. As a vegetarian on the ketogenic diet, you may have trouble meeting your protein goals every day, and protein powder is an easy addition.

Urine ketone testing

Yes, it might sound a little gross – but the best way to know for sure if you're in ketosis is to test your urine for ketones. This is a fairly common practice in the ketogenic diet, and it's much easier than you'd expect.

You can typically purchase a urine testing kit online or at a drugstore. You can expect this kit to contain testing strips and instructions that include a color-coded guide. Simply dip the test strip into your urine, and wait to see what color it turns. If it indicates your ketone levels are within the range of ketosis, congratulations! You've made it into ketosis, and you can expect to lose weight soon.

Other Pro Tips

As with every diet, the ketogenic diet has the potential to be frustrating at times. Perhaps the weight isn't coming off as quickly as you had hoped, or you're stuck on a plateau. There are several things that could be sabotaging your weight loss without you even knowing!

- **You could still be consuming too many carbohydrates.** It varies by person, but most people need to drop carbohydrate intake to just 5 to 10% of caloric intake – which is a drastic change from the typical American diet of 45 to 65% or more! In order to get an accurate picture of the amount of carbohydrates you are eating, it may be helpful to weigh or measure your food and track it in an app such as MyFitnessPal.

- **Look at what you're actually eating in a day.** Are you relying on processed foods, snacks, and desserts? What about keto-friendly convenience and fast foods? While these foods can allow you to enjoy treats and still stay in ketosis, they're contributing extra calories to your diet – which will still cause weight gain or hamper your efforts to lose weight. Try to make the majority of your diet "real food" such as full-fat dairy, avocadoes, olive oil, nuts, seeds, and eggs. Also, be sure to keep your fiber and nutrient intake up by eating plenty of non-starchy vegetables such as mushrooms, peppers, broccoli, and any kind of salad greens.

You might just be consuming too many calories each day. Just like all other diets, the ketogenic diet requires a caloric deficit in order for weight loss to occur after the initial water weight is lost. Since you are replacing carbohydrates (4 calories per gram) with fat (9 calories per gram) and keto-friendly foods tend to be higher in calories, it's extremely easy to underestimate your caloric intake. Some tips for avoiding excessive intake include snacking in moderation, getting adequate physical activity, and limiting portion sizes.

- **You could have a medical problem that you're unaware of.** This is less likely than other factors, but it's entirely possible! Some medical issues that can make it harder to lose weight and even cause weight gain include polycystic ovarian syndrome, Cushing's syndrome, hypothyroidism, or high insulin levels. If you are diagnosed with one of these problems, the ketogenic diet can still be used (often in conjunction with medication or other lifestyle changes) in order to lose weight.

- **Are you actually losing weight, just not as much as you expected?** It's easy to go into the ketogenic diet with unrealistic expectations related to weight loss. Your cousin's friend's neighbor's babysitter lost 20 pounds in their first week, right? Weight loss can be rapid and impressive at first, but sometimes it tapers off a bit or even stops for a while. Our tip is to look at the big picture here – how much have you lost overall, and how much time has that taken? Experts recommend weight loss of 1 to 3 pounds (about ½ to 1 kg) per week, so if you're in that range, you're doing great!

- **Have you started a new exercise routine** in addition to the ketogenic diet? If you're doing resistance or strength training exercises, it's entirely possible that you are losing body fat and gaining muscle. While this can slow down your weight loss somewhat, it's a healthier way to lose weight – both decreasing your risk of heart disease and strengthening your bones. If you're really bummed out by your lack of progress on the scale, take weekly measurements of your waist, arms, and thighs to get a real view of your progress.

- **Are you snacking too much?** We absolutely recommend snacking between meals (it can keep you from getting *hangry* and overdoing it at meals), but you need to be aware of the caloric content of what you're eating. Ketogenic snacks tend to be high-calorie – especially treats like fat bombs, cheese, and nut butters. If you are the kind of person who likes to snack multiple times per day (me too!) – try to find lower-calorie versions of your favorite keto-friendly snacks. Many types of jerky and nuts are lower in calories or sold in portion packs where you'll be less likely to eat several portions without noticing. Also, try snacking on keto-friendly vegetables! Veggies like celery, bell peppers, and tomatoes can be tasty snacks *and* provide you with some fiber to keep your digestion in check.

- **Are you getting enough sleep?** This possibility relates to stress. When you're stressed, your body produces more cortisol (a hormone) than usual. Cortisol tends to help the body store more fat, especially in the stomach. Stressed-out people also tend to have more sleep problems such as insomnia. Sleep deprivation has been shown to cause weight gain. Sleep problems have also been linked to affecting hormones that control hunger – such as ghrelin and leptin. Want to sleep better? Try decreasing your stress levels by meditating, or decreasing your screen time.

Hey there! Just a quick check before we continue learning further. Let me ask you – How do you feel? Are you already familiar with the concepts described here? Or, are you enjoying learning about these new ideas and methods? Please let me know. I want you to write a review on Amazon (link in the next page) and be honest about it. It will take no more than 2 minutes and would mean a lot to me. It also helps the reader community find the right books at the right time. Thank a ton.

www.bookstuff.in/veg-keto-beginners-review

- **Are you sedentary?** Yes, the ketogenic diet can help you lose weight with less effort than you might have had to put in on other diets. However, it's not magic! When you start on the ketogenic diet, you should also incorporate physical activity into your lifestyle. Exercise can not only help with weight loss, but it can also decrease the risk of developing heart disease and other chronic diseases. Additionally, when you build muscle, you're actually increasing your metabolism! If you're new to exercise, it can be intimidating to start a new routine, but we recommend creating a workout schedule of 3 to 4 days per week to start, and go when it's most convenient for you (if you're not a morning person – don't make yourself go in the morning, it won't stick!). To cut down on the excuses, try keeping a gym bag in your car for after-work exercise or setting everything out the night before a morning workout.

  This chapter was chock-full of tips and information about some of the more detailed aspects of the ketogenic diet. We discussed a few supplements that might be worth adding to your shopping list, and also went over a few reasons why you might not be getting the results you expected yet. Now, onto the recipes! Let's cook!

Chapter 8:

100 Delicious Vegetarian Keto Recipes

SOUPS

Thai Coconut Soup

Juice of ½ Lime

2 tsp Lemon grass (citronella)

2 tsp Ginger root

1½ cups canned Coconut milk

3 cups Vegetable broth

2 tsp Curry paste

14 oz Tofu (silken, firm)

2 cups Mushrooms (sliced)

2 tsp Sugar

2 tbsp Soy sauce

1 cup Red bell pepper (sliced)

Yields: 8 servings

Serving Size: ½ cup

Per Serving: 138 calories

Net Carbs: 6.1 g

Total Fat: 10.4 g

Protein: 6.2 g

Macros: 19% C | 68% F | 13% P

Ingredients

Directions

Combine lime zest, lemongrass, ginger, and coconut milk with broth in a large saucepan and bring to a boil. Reduce heat to medium-low and simmer for 5-10 minutes. Add the curry paste ½-teaspoon at a time, stirring well to combine and tasting as you go to make sure you don't make it too spicy. Stir in the tofu, mushrooms, sugar, soy sauce, and salt to taste. Simmer for about 10 more minutes. Add lime juice and serve over rice, garnished with red pepper strips and extra lime on the side.

Keto Parmesan Cauliflower Soup

Yields: 6 servings
192 calories
Net Carbs: 6.4 g
Total Fat: 16.9 g
Protein: 3.6 g
Macros: 19% C | 79% F | 2% P

Ingredients
8 tbsp Butter
Dash of Salt
Dash of Pepper
1 medium Onion
½ Leek
1 medium head Cauliflower
2 cups Water
2 tbsp Thyme (fresh)
¼ cup Parmesan cheese (grated)
1 cup Vegetable broth

Directions
Chop cauliflower, leek, thyme and onion. Set aside. Melt ¼ of butter in large pot. Add salt, onion, and leek. Cook until onion become soft and translucent. Add half of cauliflower, another 1/4 of the butter, broth, and water to pot. Bring to simmer for 10-15 minutes, until cauliflower is

tender and falling apart. Add 3/4 of remaining cauliflower to pot and continue to simmer. Melt remaining butter in a sauté pan with thyme and remaining cauliflower florets. Stir as the butter begins to bubble and brown. Once the cauliflower in the soup pot is tender, remove from heat and transfer contents of pot to a blender. Add parmesan to blender. Being careful to cover blender vent with towel, blend simmered cauliflower mixture until smooth. Add additional water to adjust consistency of soup if needed. Blend some more. Transfer blended soup to bowl. Garnish with golden florets and drizzled brown butter from sauté pan. Enjoy!

Brussels Sprouts Stew

Yields: 4 servings
Per Serving: 404 calories
Net Carbs: 9.1 g
Total Fat: 32.8 g
Protein: 10.5 g
Macros: 17% C | 73% F | 10% P

Ingredients

1 lb Brussels sprouts
1 medium Onion
1 tbsp Coconut oil
1 tsp Mustard seed
2 tbsp Cilantro (fresh)
4 cloves Garlic
2 medium Tomatoes
½ tsp Turmeric
½ tsp Cayenne pepper
2 tsp Curry powder
½ cup Cashews
1¾ cup canned Coconut milk (unsweetened)
Dash of Salt
1 Lemon

Directions

Halve brussels sprouts. Dice tomatoes. Finely dice onion. Peel and smash garlic cloves into almost a paste. Chop cilantro. Set aside. Heat half of the oil over medium heat in a wide saucepan and add mustard seeds. When they sputter, add the cilantro leaves and garlic. Sauté for about a minute. Add the onions and sauté for a minute until they begin to turn translucent. Add the tomatoes and powdered spices-- the curry powder, cayenne and turmeric. Sauté, stirring frequently, until the tomatoes release most of their liquid and get pulpy. Add the cashews, Brussels sprouts and some salt to taste. Cover the saucepan to let the Brussels sprouts get tender, around 5-8 minutes. Stir occasionally to make sure nothing's sticking to the bottom. If necessary, add a couple of tablespoons of water to the pan. Add half the coconut milk and let the sauce come to a simmer. Check if the Brussels sprouts are tender by piercing one with a fork in the center. Add the remaining coconut milk and just warm through without letting the stew boil. Check salt and add more if needed. Serve hot, with a squeeze of fresh lemon when serving.

Easy Pumpkin Soup

Per Serving: 162 calories
Net Carbs: 8.8 g
Total Fat: 12.4 g
Protein: 4.5 g
Macros: 20% C | 69% F | 11% P

Yields: 4 servings

Ingredients

2 tbsp Curry paste

4 cups Vegetable broth

1 cup canned Pumpkin

1 cup Coconut milk (canned)

1 Red bell pepper

Directions

In a large saucepan over medium heat, cook the curry paste for about 1 minute or until paste becomes fragrant. Stir in broth and pumpkin. Cook for about 3 minutes or until soup starts to bubble. Add most of the coconut milk, saving a small amount for garnish. Cook until hot, about 3 minutes. Ladle into bowls, and garnish with a drizzle of coconut milk and sliced red chilis. Garnish with cilantro leaves if desired. Serve hot.

Pea Soup with Mint

Yields: 8 servings

Per Serving: 234 calories

Net Carbs: 14.3 g

Total Fat: 14.5 g

Protein: 7.2 g

Macros: 32% C | 56% F | 12% P

Ingredients

1 cup Heavy whipping cream

7 cups Green peas (frozen)

1 small Onion

2 tbsp Butter

1 cup Spearmint (fresh)

5 cups Vegetable broth

Directions

Finely chop onion. In a 4-quart heavy saucepan, cook onion in butter with salt to taste over moderately low heat, stirring occasionally, until softened. Add peas and 3 cups broth and simmer, uncovered, until peas are tender, 5 to 7 minutes. Stir in mint and remaining 2 cups broth and remove pan from heat. In a blender purée soup in batches until very smooth (use caution when blending hot liquids), forcing each batch through a sieve into a large bowl. (Discard solids in sieve between batches.) Whisk in cream (or cream-yogurt mixture) and salt and pepper to taste. If serving soup cold, chill, covered. If serving soup hot, reheat but do not let boil.

Cabbage & Tofu Soup

Ingredients

1 package Tofu (firm)

1 cup Cabbage (chopped)

1 Italian tomato

1 cup Eggplant (cubed)

½ medium Onion

3 cloves Garlic (minced)

2 cups Vegetable broth

1 tbsp Olive oil

Yields: 4 servings

Per Serving: 103 calories

Net Carbs: 5.1 g

Total Fat: 4.8 g

Protein: 8.5 g

Macros: 25% C | 42% F | 33% P

Directions

Simmer onion, garlic, and olive oil until onions are translucent. Add remaining ingredients, and let simmer for about 20 minutes. Add salt and pepper to taste. Serve hot.

Tomato & Roasted Red Pepper Soup

Yields: 4 servings
Per Serving: 147 calories
Net Carbs: 8.2 g
Total Fat: 10.6 g
Protein: 2.3 g
Macros: 29% C | 65% F | 6% P

Ingredients

3 cups Red bell pepper (sliced)
4 medium Tomatoes
3 cloves Garlic
3 tbsp Olive oil
Dash of Salt
Dash of Pepper
2 tbsp Rosemary (fresh)
1 tbsp Thyme (fresh)
¼ cup Vegetable broth
¼ cup Tomato puree
2 tbsp Vinegar

Directions

Preheat oven to 375 F. Chop peppers into quarters and remove the center. Slice tomatoes and place onto a rimmed baking sheet with bell peppers and garlic. Drizzle generously with olive oil and sprinkle with salt and pepper. Scatter rosemary and thyme over the vegetables. Roast in the oven for 35-40 minutes. Transfer everything on the pan to a blender or food processor. Add the broth, tomato purée, and apple cider vinegar. Purée until smooth, adding more broth if necessary to reach desired consistency. Adjust salt and pepper to taste. Ladle into bowls and serve warm.

Asparagus Soup

Macros: 36% C | 52% F | 12% P

Ingredients

4 tsp Pepper (ground)

1 lb Asparagus

1 cup Milk (reduced-fat)

1 tsp Garlic powder

1 cup Vegetable broth

1 medium Onion

2 tbsp Butter

Yields: 4 servings

Per Serving: 124 calories

Net Carbs: 8.2 g

Total Fat: 7.1 g

Protein: 5.5 g

Directions

Chop onion. Trim and coarsely chop asparagus. Microwave onion and butter on HIGH for 2 minutes. Add asparagus, vegetable broth, garlic powder and white pepper. Microwave, covered, on HIGH for 10 to 12 minutes. Puree in blender. Return mixture to microwave-safe dish, stir in milk and microwave until heated through. Serve warm.

Creamy Broccoli Soup

Yields: 4 servings
Per Serving: 68 calories
Net Carbs: 3.1 g

Total Fat: 4.9 g
Protein: 1.9 g
Macros: 32% C | 65% F | 3% P

Ingredients
1 large stalk Broccoli
Dash of Salt
Dash of Pepper
2 tsp Olive oil
4 tbsp Sour cream

Directions

Place Pot on stove, add enough water to barely cover the tops of broccoli chunks when added. Heat on high to just before a rolling boil. Add salt. Chop stalk and florets into manageable chunks while water heats. Add broccoli chunks and wait a minute or so until water returns to boil, reduce heat to medium. Watch to make sure water keeps a gentle boil for a moment. Place lid on and time to 5-7 minutes. Once broccoli is tender and bright green, drain and set aside reserving the liquid. Place broccoli in blender. Pour hot broccoli water stock about 1/3 of the way up to the top of the broccoli chunks. Pulse blend on low momentarily until homogenized. Set aside leftover broccoli stock to use in another recipe. Add more stock if necessary and increase blending until pureed and smooth. Add salt, pepper, and olive oil and mix to combine. Serve while hot with a dollop of sour cream.

Savory Mushroom Soup

Macros: 29% C | 62% F | 9% P

<u>Ingredients</u>
1 can (10.7 oz) Cream of mushroom soup
3 tbsp Sour cream
¼ medium Onion
1 cup Milk (reduced-fat)
1½ tbsp Butter
½ cup Peas

Yields: 3 servings
Per Serving: 212 calories
Net Carbs: 13.4 g
Total Fat: 14.6 g
Protein: 5.8 g

<u>Directions</u>
Mince onion. In small saucepan saute onion in butter. Add soup, milk, and peas. Heat on medium-low until peas are soft. Add sour cream. Stir. When hot, serve. Add sour cream to desired thickness.

Avocado Cucumber Soup

Yields: 2 servings
Per Serving: 115 calories
Net Carbs: 5.2 g
Total Fat: 7.8 g
Protein: 2.7 g
Macros: 30% C | 61% F | 9% P

Ingredients

2 large Cucumbers

½ Avocado

1 tsp Lemon juice

1 tsp Dill (fresh)

1 tbsp Cilantro (fresh)

Directions

Blend all the ingredients in a food processor or blender. Serve cold.

SALADS

Cucumber Walnut Salad

Yields: 2 servings
Per Serving: 191 calories
Net Carbs: 5 g

Total Fat: 16.8 g
Protein: 4.4 g
Macros: 12% C | 79% F | 9% P

Ingredients
5¼ cup Lettuce (shredded)
2 medium Cucumbers
1 tbsp Olive oil
Dash of Salt
Dash of Pepper
¼ cup Walnuts (chopped)

Directions
Add lettuce to a bowl. Peel, slice, and add cucumbers. Add olive oil, season with salt and pepper, and mix. Crush and add walnuts. Serve immediately.

Simple Arugula Salad

Yields: 3 servings
Per Serving: 130 calories
Net Carbs: 1.9 g
Total Fat: 11.7 g
Protein: 4.3 g
Macros: 6% C | 81% F | 13% P

Ingredients

2 Plum tomatoes

3 cups Arugula

2 tsp Red wine vinegar

¼ cup Parmesan cheese (grated)

2 tbsp Olive oil

Directions

Mix tomatoes, arugula, and vinegar in a small bowl. Using a wooden spoon, slowly mix in oil, then Parmesan. Serve cold.

Green Pea Salad

Protein: 10.3 g
Macros: 23% C | 62% F | 15% P

Ingredients

1 can Peas

4 oz Cheddar cheese

2 tbsp Onions (chopped)

1 tbsp Sugar

4 tbsp Mayonnaise

Yields: 4 servings
Per Serving: 273 calories
Net Carbs: 10.5 g
Total Fat: 18.9 g

Directions

In a medium serving bowl, mix together peas, cheese, and onion. Stir in sugar and mayonnaise. Chill for at least 1 hour before serving.

Blue Cheese Salad

Total Fat: 17.1 g
Protein: 12.8 g
Macros: 15% C | 64% F | 21% P

<u>Ingredients</u>
2 cups Lettuce (shredded)
½ cup Cherry tomatoes
2 tbsp Italian dressing
3 oz Blue cheese

Yields: 1 serving
Per Serving: 240 calories
Net Carbs: 7.3 g

<u>Directions</u>
Gently mix the ingredients in a bowl. Serve cold.

Shaved Fennel Salad

Protein: 6.9 g
Macros: 16% C | 76% F | 8% P

<u>Ingredients</u>
2 tbsp Olive oil
2 tbsp Parmesan cheese
1 tbsp Lemon juice
1 bulb Fennel
1 tbsp Parsley
⅛ tsp Thyme (fresh)

Yields: 1 serving
Per Serving: 357 calories
Net Carbs: 11.2 g
Total Fat: 30.3 g

Directions

In a salad bowl, combine all ingredients and gently toss until well incorporated. Serve immediately.

Tomato-Onion Salad

Total Fat: 7.1 g
Protein: 1.8 g
Macros: 28% C | 65% F | 7% P

Ingredients

3 medium Tomatoes
2 tbsp Onions (chopped)
Dash of Salt
1 tbsp Olive oil
1 tbsp Lemon juice

Yields: 2 servings
Per Serving: 99 calories
Net Carbs: 6.2 g

Directions

Place the chopped tomatoes, onions, salt, olive oil, and lemon juice in a bowl. Toss together well. Serve cold.

Red Leaf Vinaigrette Salad

Total Fat: 6.8 g

Protein: 0.5 g

Macros: 7% C | 90% F | 3% P

Ingredients

8 cups Lettuce (shredded)

½ tsp Salt

½ cup + 1 tbsp Olive oil

2 tbsp Vinegar

½ tsp Pepper

4 cups Radicchio (shredded)

Yields: 10 servings

Per Serving: 68 calories

Net Carbs: 0.9 g

Directions

Whisk together vinegar, salt, and pepper in a large bowl, then add oil in a slow stream, whisking until emulsified. Add lettuces and greens and toss to coat. Serve immediately.

Lemon-Parmesan Salad

Yields: 1 serving

Per Serving: 169 calories

Net Carbs: 3.3 g

Total Fat: 15.3 g

Protein: 3.4 g

Macros: 10% C | 82% F | 8% P

Ingredients

3 cups Lettuce (shredded)

1 tbsp Olive oil

¼ tsp Lemon juice

Dash of Salt

Dash of Pepper

1 tsp Garlic

1 tbsp Parmesan cheese (grated)

Directions

Chop lettuce into bite-sized pieces. Combine remaining ingredients in a blender until smooth. Pour over lettuce. Serve cold.

Pecan-Celeriac Salad

Macros: 6% C | 90% F | 4% P

Ingredients

1 cup Celeriac (celery root)

½ tsp Salt

3 tbsp Vinegar

¾ tsp Pepper

¼ cup Parsley (fresh)

¼ cup Olive oil

1 cup Pecans (halved)

2 tbsp Shallots (chopped)

Yields: 8 servings

Per Serving: 157 calories

Net Carbs: 2.5 g

Total Fat: 15.7 g

Protein: 1.6 g

Directions

Toast and then cool pecans. Peel and chop celery root. Chop parsley. Finely chop shallot. Finely chop 2/3 of nuts. Coarsely grate celery root in a food processor fitted with medium shredding disk. Stir together vinegar, salt, and pepper in a large bowl until salt is dissolved, then add celery root, chopped nuts, parsley, and shallot and toss well. Drizzle salad with oil and toss again. Serve sprinkled with remaining pecans.

Avocado-Radish Chopped Salad

Yields: 2 servings
Per Serving: 272 calories
Net Carbs: 7.7 g
Total Fat: 24.4 g
Protein: 3 g
Macros: 15% C | 81% F | 4% P

Ingredients

1 Avocado
5 medium Radishes
½ small Onion
1 large Cucumber
Juice of 1 lemon
2 tbsp Olive oil
1 clove Garlic (minced)
1 tbsp Shallots (chopped)
Dash of Salt
Dash of Pepper
¼ cup Parsley (fresh)

Directions

Chop the avocado, radishes, onion, and cucumber. Set aside. Make the dressing by combining the lemon juice, olive oil, minced garlic, minced shallots, salt and pepper in a large bowl. Mix thoroughly. Add the chopped avocado, radish, onion and cucumber to the bowl. Toss with the dressing until everything is evenly coated. Add more salt and pepper if desired, garnish with parsley, and then serve.

Sesame Tofu Salad

Yields: 4 servings
Per Serving: 187 calories
Net Carbs: 2.6 g
Total Fat: 14.7 g
Protein: 11 g

Macros: 5% C | 71% F | 24% P

Ingredients
4 tsp Soy sauce
¾ block Tofu (firm)
2 tbsp Vegetable oil
2 tsp Rice wine vinegar
¾ tsp Sesame oil
4 large stalks Celery
2 tsp Sesame seeds
½ tsp Pepper

Directions

Rinse tofu and pat dry, then cut crosswise into 1/4-inch-thick slices. Arrange slices in 1 layer on a triple thickness of paper towels, then cover with another triple thickness of paper towels. Put a small baking sheet on top of tofu and weight with 3 (1-lb) cans (this removes excess moisture) for 10 minutes. Meanwhile, whisk together oils, vinegar, soy sauce, and pepper in a large bowl. Trim celery, then peel with a vegetable peeler and slice very thin diagonally. Cut tofu crosswise into 1/4-inch-wide sticks and transfer to a bowl. Toss gently with dressing, celery, sesame seeds, and salt to taste.

Tomato & Avocado Salad

Yields: 1 serving

Per Serving: 344 calories

Net Carbs: 7.6 g

Total Fat: 29.7 g

Protein: 5 g

Macros: 16% C | 78% F | 6% P

<u>Ingredients</u>

1 Avocado

Dash of Pepper

Dash of Salt

½ Lemon

½ cup Cherry tomatoes

<u>Directions</u>

Dice avocado. Squeeze half of lemon over top. Add ground salt and pepper. Dice tomatoes into halves and combine with avocado. Serve cold.

Quick Tofu Salad

Per Serving: 265 calories

Net Carbs: 17.3 g

Total Fat: 16.4 g

Protein: 9.3 g

Macros: 30% C | 56% F | 14% P)

Yields: 1 serving

Ingredients

2 cups Lettuce (shredded)

½ cup Cherry tomatoes

1 slice (84 g) Tofu (firm)

1 tbsp Olive oil

1 cup Onions (chopped)

Directions

Gently mix the ingredients in a bowl. Serve cold.

Gouda-Broccoli Salad

Yields: 4 servings

Per Serving: 362 calories

Net Carbs: 7.8 g

Total Fat: 28.2 g

Protein: 18.6 g

Macros: 9% C | 70% F | 21% P

Ingredients

3 cups Broccoli (florets)

¼ cup Onions (chopped)

4 oz Grape tomatoes

½ cup Almonds (sliced)

8 oz Gouda cheese

2 tbsp Olive oil

⅓ cup Red wine vinegar

¼ tsp Sugar

¼ tsp Pepper

Dash of Salt

Directions

Cook broccoli in boiling salted water for 1 minute. Drain well; rinse with cold water; drain well again. Combine the broccoli with onion, tomatoes, nuts, and cheese. In a small bowl, whisk together oil, vinegar, sugar, pepper and salt; pour over salad mixture and toss to coat. Serve cool.

BEVERAGES

Chocolate Avocado Shake

Protein: 31.1 g
Macros: 14% C | 52% F | 34% P

Ingredients
½ cup Soymilk (unsweetened)
1 scoop (30 g) Protein powder
½ Avocado
½ tbsp Flaxseed (whole)
⅓ tbsp Chia seeds

Yields: 1 serving
Per Serving: 368 calories
Net Carbs: 6.8 g
Total Fat: 21.1 g

Directions
Combine all ingredients in a blender and pulse until smooth. Add more liquid if necessary. Serve cold.

Banana-Coconut Shake

Per Serving: 485 calories
Net Carbs: 27.4 g
Total Fat: 29.9 g
Protein: 27.9 g
Macros: 22% C | 55% F | 23% P

Yields: 1 serving

Ingredients

1 scoop (30 g) Protein powder

½ cup Coconut milk

15 g frozen Orange juice concentrate

½ cup Banana (sliced)

Directions

Mix the protein powder with the coconut milk, orange juice and frozen banana. Add a few ice cubes. Mix everything together in blender.

Tropical Blueberry Smoothie

Yields: 1 serving
Per Serving: 649 calories
Net Carbs: 24.8 g
Total Fat: 53.2 g
Protein: 15.9 g
Macros: 16% C | 74% F | 10% P

Ingredients

4 oz Greek yogurt (nonfat)

⅔ cup Coconut milk

1½ tsp Vanilla extract

3 Ice cubes

1 tbsp Coconut oil

1 cup Blueberries (frozen)

Directions

Blend everything except coconut oil. Slowly pour coconut oil in while blender is running. Pour into a glass, garnish with some dried coconut or a fresh strawberry if desired, and serve cold.

Creamy Avocado Shake

Yields: 2 servings
Per Serving: 456 calories
Net Carbs: 6.7 g

Total Fat: 39.2 g
Protein: 11.5 g
Macros: 13% C | 77% F | 10% P

Ingredients

4 oz Almond milk

1 Avocado

3 oz Greek yogurt

2 Ice cubes

Directions

Combine all ingredients in a blender and pulse until smooth. Serve cold.

Strawberry Cottage Shake

Protein: 40.5 g
Macros: 27% C | 10% F | 63% P

Ingredients
½ cup Cottage cheese
½ cup Strawberries (whole)
1 scoop (30 g) Protein powder
¼ cup Milk (lowfat)
½ tsp Vanilla extract
1 cup Ice cubes

Yields: 1 serving
Per Serving: 256 calories
Net Carbs: 13.5 g
Total Fat: 2.9 g

Directions
Combine all ingredients in a blender and pulse until smooth. Serve cold.

Peanut Butter Protein Shake

Per Serving: 410 calories
Net Carbs: 18.7 g
Total Fat: 19.5 g
Protein: 34.2 g
Macros: 24% C | 43% F | 33% P

Yields: 1 serving

Ingredients

1 scoop (30 g) Protein powder

½ cup Almond milk

½ tbsp Chia seeds

⅓ large Banana

1 tbsp Peanut butter

1 tbsp Coconut meat

3 tbsp Greek yogurt

Directions

Combine all ingredients in a blender and pulse until smooth.

Mean Green Protein Smoothie

Yields: 2 servings

Per Serving: 147 calories

Net Carbs: 6.1 g

Total Fat: 6.3 g

Protein: 14.5 g

Macros: 22% C | 39% F | 39% P

Ingredients

1½ cups Water

1 scoop (30 g) Protein powder

2 slices Ginger root (1")

½ cup Celery (chopped)

½ cup Cucumber (sliced)

½ cup Avocado (cubed)

1 cup Kale (chopped)

1 cup Spinach (chopped)

Directions

Combine all ingredients in a blender and pulse until smooth.

Mocha Protein Shake

Yields: 1 serving

Per Serving: 446 calories

Net Carbs: 20.3 g

Total Fat: 7.5 g

Protein: 72.2 g

Macros: 20% C | 15% F | 65% P

Ingredients

1 cup Milk (reduced-fat)

2⅔ scoops (80 g) Protein powder

2 tbsp Water

4 Ice cubes

6 fl oz Coffee

Directions

Combine all ingredients in a blender and pulse until smooth.

Avocado-Lime Smoothie

Protein: 6.5 g

Macros: 22% C | 70% F | 8% P

Ingredients

1 cup Whole milk

1 Avocado

¼ cup Coconut milk

1 cup Ice cubes

1½ tbsp Lime juice

1 tbsp Sugar

Yields: 2 servings

Per Serving: 318 calories

Net Carbs: 15.7 g

Total Fat: 24.8 g

Directions

Chill two glasses while you prepare your smoothie. Remove the seed and skin from the avocado cut in 4 pieces and into a blender. Add milk, lime juice and sugar to the blender; purée. Then add 1 cup ice; purée until smooth. Divide between 2 chilled glasses and serve.

Peanut Butter-Flax Shake

Yields: 1 serving

Per Serving: 374 calories

Net Carbs: 6.8 g

Total Fat: 24.7 g

Protein: 30.1 g

Macros: 9% C | 59% F | 32% P

Ingredients

1 scoop (30 g) Protein powder

2 tbsp Heavy whipping cream

1 tbsp Peanut butter

1 tbsp Flaxseed (whole)

1½ cups Water

Directions

Mix the protein powder along with the cream, peanut butter and flaxseed in water. Add ice cubes. Blend everything in mixer.

APPETIZERS

Sesame Tempeh Sticks

Yields: 4 servings
Per Serving: 432 calories
Net Carbs: 20.3 g
Total Fat: 28.4 g
Protein: 26.7 g
Macros: 16% C | 59% F | 25% P

Ingredients

16 oz Tempeh
¼ cup Almond milk
2 tbsp Mayonnaise
½ tbsp Dijon mustard
½ tsp Red pepper flakes
¼ tsp Pepper
¼ tsp Garlic powder
4 tbsp Sesame seeds
⅛ cup Panko Breadcrumbs
¼ cup Soy sauce
2 tbsp Sesame butter
Juice of 1 lime
2 tsp Honey
1 medium Scallion

Directions

Preheat oven to 350 F and line a baking sheet with wax paper or aluminum foil. Remove tempeh blocks from packages and slice into equal-sized stick pieces. In a small bowl, combine almond milk, mayo, dijon mustard, 1 tbsp soy sauce, 1/4 tbs red pepper flakes, pepper, and garlic powder. Whisk until well combined. In a separate small bowl, add the sesame seeds and panko breadcrumbs. Dip the tempeh sticks into the liquid mixture and then pour the sesame seeds over the sticks with your fingers to stick to the mixture. Continue until all the sticks are covered. Transfer to the lined baking sheet and bake for 15 minutes. While the tempeh is baking, prepare the dipping sauce: In a small bowl, combine 1/4 cup soy sauce, 2 tbsp tahini, juice from 1 lime, 2 tsp honey, dashes of red pepper flakes, salt and pepper. Allow the tempeh to cool for a couple minutes before serving. Serve with the dipping sauce.

Keto-Style Creamed Spinach

Macros: 19% C | 52% F | 29% P

Ingredients

10 oz Spinach (frozen)

3 tbsp Parmesan cheese

3 tbsp Cream cheese

2 tbsp Sour cream

¼ tsp Garlic powder

¼ tsp Onion powder

Dash of Salt

Dash of Pepper

Yields: 2 servings

Per Serving: 140 calories

Net Carbs: 5.1 g

Total Fat: 8.1 g

Protein: 10.3 g

Directions

Defrost frozen spinach in the microwave. Add to a pan on medium-high heat and let excess water boil off. Add seasoning and cream cheese to the pan. Stir together until cream cheese has melted. Add sour cream and parmesan and mix together well until the creamed spinach is thickened. Serve immediately.

Keto NO-tato Salad

Yields: 4 servings
Per Serving: 143 calories
Net Carbs: 10 g
Total Fat: 7.4 g
Protein: 7.5 g
Macros: 32% C | 47% F | 21% P

<u>Ingredients</u>
1 large head Cauliflower
2 large Eggs
⅓ cup Mayonnaise
1 tsp Mustard
1 tbsp Relish
1 tbsp Onions (chopped)
1 tsp Dill (fresh)
1 tsp Chives (chopped)
1 tsp Vinegar
½ tsp Salt
½ tsp Pepper
½ tsp Paprika

<u>Directions</u>
Hard boil eggs: Place your eggs in a pot and cover completely with cold water by 1 inch. Bring to a boil over medium-high heat, then cover, remove from the heat and set aside for 10 minutes. Drain, cool in ice water and peel. Cut the cauliflower into bite sized pieces, much like you would a potato for potato salad. Rinse and drain. Add just enough water to cover the bottom of a 12-inch skillet and bring to a boil over medium high heat. Add the cauliflower to the skillet and cover to steam. Let steam for 3-5 minutes, checking for doneness with a fork.

When a fork slides in easily, add the cauliflower to a large bowl. Do not overcook the cauliflower or your salad will be mushy. Chop the hard-boiled eggs into small pieces and add to the bowl with the cauliflower. In a small bowl, combine the remaining ingredients, except for the paprika, and whisk together to form the dressing for the salad. Gently fold the dressing into the cauliflower and eggs, stirring to coat each piece. Sprinkle with paprika. Refrigerate for at least 1 hour or until cold.

Garlic Sesame Eggplant

Ingredients
1 Eggplant (peeled)
½ tsp Salt
2 tbsp Butter
2 cloves Garlic (minced)
½ cup Water
2 tbsp Soy sauce
¼ tsp Ginger
1 tbsp Sesame oil
2 tbsp Sesame seeds

Yields: 4 servings
Per Serving: 159 calories
Net Carbs: 5 g
Total Fat: 13 g
Protein: 3.2 g
Macros: 18% C | 74% F | 8% P

Directions
Cube eggplant into 1/2 inch cubes and place in large colander or sieve set over a large bowl. Sprinkle eggplant generously with salt, mixing to combine, and let drain at least one hour. Heat the butter in a large skillet over medium heat until melted and froth is beginning to subside.

Sauté eggplant until soft, 5 to 7 minutes. Add garlic and sauté until fragrant, about 30 seconds. In a small bowl, whisk together water, soy sauce and ground ginger. Add to skillet and stir until eggplant is well coated. Remove from heat and stir in sesame oil and toasted sesame seeds.

Baked Goat Cheese Portobella Caps

Net Carbs: 4.9 g
Total Fat: 8.6 g
Protein: 7.7 g
Macros: 15% C | 61% F | 24% P

Ingredients
½ cup Tomato sauce
2 Portobella mushrooms (whole)
1¾ oz Goat cheese (soft)
1 tbsp Pine nuts
½ tbsp Basil (fresh, chopped)

Yields: 2 servings
Per Serving: 127 calories

Directions
Preheat the oven to 375 F. Spread the sauce in the bottom of a 9" X 9" baking dish. Arrange the mushroom caps, gill side up, on top. Place a piece of goat cheese on each mushroom. Sprinkle evenly with the pine nuts. Bake for 30 minutes, or until hot and bubbly. Top with the chopped basil.

Cheesy Zucchini Patties

Yields: 12 servings
Per Serving: 93 calories
Net Carbs: 5.1 g
Total Fat: 5.7 g
Protein: 5 g
Macros: 23% C | 55% F | 22% P

Ingredients

½ cup Wheat flour

2 tbsp Vegetable oil

¼ cup Onions (chopped)

½ cup Mozzarella cheese (shredded)

1 tsp Salt

½ cup Parmesan cheese (grated)

2 cups Zucchini (mashed)

2 extra large Eggs

Directions

Grate zucchinis. Beat eggs. Chop onion. In a medium bowl, combine the zucchini, eggs, onion, flour, Parmesan cheese, mozzarella cheese, and salt. Stir well enough to distribute ingredients evenly. Heat a small amount of oil in a skillet over medium-high heat. Drop zucchini mixture by heaping tablespoonfuls, and cook for a few minutes on each side until golden. Serve warm.

Deviled Eggs

Yields: 12 servings
Per Serving: 109 calories
Net Carbs: 3.2 g

Total Fat: 7.2 g
Protein: 7.3 g
Macros: 14% C | 59% F | 27% P

Ingredients
12 large Eggs
⅓ cup Ranch dressing
½ cup Cream cheese
½ cup Onions (chopped)
1 large Pickle (chopped)

Directions

Place eggs in a large saucepan and cover with cold water. Bring water to a boil and immediately remove from heat. Cover and let eggs stand in hot water for 10 to 12 minutes. Remove from hot water, cool and peel. Slice eggs in half lengthwise and remove yolks. Place yolks in a medium bowl. Mash together with ranch-style salad dressing. Mix in the cream cheese, then the onion and dill pickle. Fill the hollowed egg whites generously with the egg yolk mixture. Chill in the refrigerator until serving.

Cheesy Mashed Cauliflower

Protein: 4.3 g
Macros: 4% C | 84% F | 12% P

Ingredients
¼ medium head Cauliflower
2 tbsp Heavy whipping cream
2 tbsp Butter
2 oz Cheddar cheese (shredded)
Dash of Salt
Dash of Pepper

Yields: 4 servings
Per Serving: 144 calories
Net Carbs: 1.5 g
Total Fat: 13.4 g

Directions
Wash and trim the cauliflower, breaking it into medium sized pieces. Place in a microwave safe bowl with 2 tbsp of cream and 1 tbsp of butter. Microwave, uncovered, on high for 6 minutes. Stir to coat cauliflower with cream/butter mixture. Microwave for another 6 minutes on high. Remove from the microwave and put into a high-speed blender or food processor along with the cheese. Purée until smooth. Season with salt and pepper to taste. Adjust the cream and butter to your preference. Serve warm.

ENTREES

Vegan Peanut Lettuce Wraps

Yields: 4 servings
Per Serving: 373 calories
Net Carbs: 15.3 g
Total Fat: 26.8 g
Protein: 16.3 g
Macros: 18% C | 65% F | 17% P

Ingredients

4 leaves Lettuce (outer)
1 large Red bell pepper
2 large Carrots
2 medium Cucumbers
12 oz Tofu (silken, firm)
4 sprigs Cilantro (fresh)
½ cup Peanut butter
2 tbsp Sesame oil
1½ tbsp Soy sauce
1 tsp Sugar
2 cloves Garlic (minced)
Juice of 1 lime
¼ tsp Red pepper flakes
1 tsp Coconut oil

Directions

Coat grill pan with coconut oil. Drain tofu, slice in half, and press with cloth until dry. Squeeze out as much moisture as possible. Grill tofu for 5 minutes on each side, or until crispy. Remove from heat and slice into strips. To create the peanut dipping sauce: combine peanut butter, sesame oil, soy sauce, garlic, juice of 1 lime, sugar, and red pepper flakes. Mix well. Add water to achieve desired consistency and additional salt to taste. To prepare vegetables: use a julienne peeler, creating vegetable noodles out of carrots and cucumbers. If you don't have a peeler, you can cut these into thin strips. De-seed and cut bell pepper into match sticks, wash and chop cilantro, rinse and dry lettuce leaves. Layer tofu, bell pepper, carrots, cilantro and cucumber in cabbage leaves and roll up! Either dip into the peanut sauce, or use the peanut sauce or toothpicks to secure leaves if necessary.

Chik'n Avocado Salad

Ingredients

2 cups Quorn Chik'n Tenders (or similar)

2 Avocado

2 tbsp Lime juice

¼ cup Scallions (chopped)

½ cup Cilantro (fresh)

2 tbsp Mayonnaise (light)

Yields: 5 servings
Per Serving: 144 calories
Net Carbs: 4.2 g
Total Fat: 10.5 g
Protein: 5.2 g
Macros: 20% C | 66% F | 14% P

Directions

Heat oil in a sauté pan over medium heat. Add chik'n tenders and sauté for about 14 minutes; set aside. Dice the avocados, and toss with 1 tbsp of the lime juice. Slice the scallion. Finely chop the cilantro. Mix mayonnaise and remaining 1 tbsp lime juice to make the dressing. Put the 2 cups of chik'n tenders pieces in a mixing bowl, and add the sliced green onions and dressing. Mix well. Add the avocado, mix and combine. Add the chopped cilantro and mix again until it's just barely combined. Serve right away or chill.

Spicy Peanut Butter Tofu

Ingredients

16 oz Tofu (extra firm)

3 tbsp Soy sauce

3 tbsp Rice wine vinegar

2 tbsp Peanut butter

1 tbsp Agave nectar

2 tbsp Water

6 tsp Sriracha sauce

3 cloves Garlic

1 tbsp Ginger (grated)

2 stalks Scallions

1 tbsp Peanut oil

Yields: 4 servings
Per Serving: 221 calories
Net Carbs: 10.9 g
Total Fat: 14.2 g
Protein: 14.6 g
Macros: 16% C | 58% F | 26% P

Directions

Drain tofu well in a colander placed in the sink, then press to remove as much liquid as possible. Cut tofu into lengthwise strips about 1" wide. Whisk together the soy sauce, rice vinegar, peanut butter, agave, stock or water, and then add the sriracha. Cut the pieces of garlic and ginger, and diagonally slice green onions. Heat a dry wok (or heavy pan) over high heat for 1 minute, then add the peanut oil and heat about 30 seconds more. Add the sliced pieces of ginger and garlic and cook just until they are fragrant (about 30 seconds); then remove and discard. Add tofu pieces, lower heat to medium-high and cook, turning often, until the tofu is nicely browned on both sides, about 7-8 minutes. When all the tofu pieces are browned, add the sauce, turn heat to low, and cook just until the sauce thickens slightly and coats the tofu. Don't cook too long, or the sauce will get too thick and won't pour correctly. Remove pan from the heat, transfer tofu pieces to a plate and pour sauce over and garnish with green onion slices. Serve hot.

Keto Sauerkraut-Egg Salad

Total Fat: 20.8 g
Protein: 20.6 g
Macros: 12% C | 61% F | 27% P

<u>Ingredients</u>
6 large Eggs
¼ cup Mayonnaise
½ cup Sauerkraut
Dash of Salt
Dash of Pepper
3 cups Spinach (fresh)

Yields: 2 servings
Per Serving: 305 calories
Net Carbs: 6.6 g

<u>Directions</u>
Hard boil eggs: place in a sauce pan on medium-high heat and fill with water so the eggs are totally covered by about 1". When the water begins to boil, cover the pan and remove from heat (turn off the stove).

Wait 10 minutes. Carefully drain the water and cool the eggs by running cold water over them. When the eggs are cool enough to handle, peel them. Toss peeled eggs in a bowl, and chop to desired size using a fork or pastry cutter. Add mayo, drained sauerkraut, and salt and pepper to taste. Serve on a bed of spinach.

Cauliflower Risotto

Yields: 6 servings
Per Serving: 209 calories
Net Carbs: 8.7 g
Total Fat: 15.6 g
Protein: 6.6 g
Macros: 20% C | 67% F | 13% P

<u>Ingredients</u>
3 tbsp Olive oil
4½ cups Mushrooms (whole)
1 medium head Cauliflower
2 fl oz White wine
1 cup Onions (chopped)
2 cloves Garlic (minced)
½ cup Vegetable broth
6 tbsp Pine nuts
2 tbsp Nutritional yeast
1 tsp Salt
2 tbsp Butter
Dash of Pepper
⅓ tbsp White truffle oil

<u>Directions</u>
Grate cauliflower by hand or using a food processor. Set aside. Mince onion and garlic. Chop mushrooms. Set aside. Heat 1/3 of olive oil in a medium skillet and cook the mushrooms until tender; set aside. Heat the rest of the olive oil in a large skillet over medium heat and cook the

onions and garlic for a few minutes until the onion becomes translucent. Add the cauliflower and wine, and cook for about 5 minutes, until the wine has evaporated. Add the broth, reduce heat and cover, letting it cook a few minutes. You'll want the cauliflower to be "al dente" with a little texture so it isn't just mush. Meanwhile, pulse together the pine nuts, nutritional yeast, and salt in a food processor until it forms a powdery consistency. Remove the cauliflower from the heat and stir in the nut mixture until well combined. Stir in the butter and season with pepper, to taste. Stir in the mushrooms and drizzle some truffle oil on top before serving.

Vegetarian Tikka Masala

Yields: 5 servings
Serving Size: 1⅔ cups
Per Serving: 362 calories
Net Carbs: 21.7 g
Total Fat: 21.5 g
Protein: 22.2 g
Macros: 22% C | 53% F | 25% P

Ingredients
9 tsp Garam masala
1 tsp Turmeric
¾ tsp Salt
¼ tsp Red pepper flakes (crushed)
32 oz Tofu (extra firm)
3 tbsp Canola oil
1 Onion
1 small Red bell pepper
1 tbsp Ginger root
2 cloves Garlic (minced)
1 tbsp Wheat flour
2 (15oz) cans Tomatoes (crushed)
⅓ cup Half and half

Directions

Combine garam masala, turmeric, salt and crushed red pepper in a small bowl. Cut tofu into 1-inch cubes and blot dry with paper towels. Toss the tofu in a medium bowl with 1 tbsp of the spice mixture. Heat 1 tbsp oil in a large nonstick skillet over medium-high heat. Add the tofu and cook, stirring every 2 minutes, until browned, 8 to 10 minutes. Transfer to a plate. Add the remaining 2 tbsp oil, onion, bell pepper, ginger and garlic and cook, stirring often, until starting to brown, 5 to 7 minutes. Add flour and the remaining spice mix; stir until fragrant and coated, about 1 minute. Add tomatoes, bring to a simmer and cook, stirring often, until the vegetables are tender, 3 to 5 minutes more. Return the tofu to the pan; cook, stirring, until heated through, about 2 minutes. Remove from heat and stir in half-and-half.

Sweet Potatoes & Mustard-Crusted Tofu

Yields: 4 servings
Per Serving: 361 calories
Net Carbs: 17.5 g
Total Fat: 23.7 g
Protein: 19 g
Macros: 20% C | 59% F | 21% P

Ingredients

4 tbsp Vegetable oil
1 tbsp Ginger root
8 cups Kale (chopped)

½ medium Onion

½ cup Dijon mustard

1 block (16 oz) Tofu (extra firm)

2 tbsp Lime juice

1 Sweet potato (about 5" long)

Directions

Peel and mince ginger. Chop kale, onion, and sweet potato. Cut tofu into 8 ½"-thick slices. Arrange on paper towels; drain 10 minutes. Spread both sides of each slice with mustard. Heat 2 tbsp oil in large nonstick skillet over medium-high heat. Add onion and ginger; sauté 1 minute. Add kale, sweet potato, and lime juice. Cover, reduce heat to low, and cook until potato is tender and kale is wilted, about 12 minutes. Meanwhile, heat remaining 2 tbsp oil in another large nonstick skillet over medium heat. Add tofu; cover and cook until heated through and crisp, about 2 minutes per side (some mustard seeds may fall off tofu). Arrange kale and sweet potato mixture on plate. Overlap tofu slices atop vegetables and serve.

Broccoli Alfredo Pizza

Yields: 4 servings

Per Serving: 336 calories

Net Carbs: 2.3 g

Total Fat: 30.3 g

Protein: 13.6 g

Macros: 3% C | 81% F | 16% P

Ingredients

1 tbsp Olive oil

1 cup Italian blend cheese

1 cup Mozzarella cheese

2 oz Mascarpone cheese

2 tbsp Clarified butter (ghee)

1 tbsp Heavy whipping cream

1 tsp Garlic (minced)

⅛ tsp Lemon pepper

Dash of Salt

⅓ cup Broccoli (chopped)

Directions

Chop broccoli. Quickly steam in microwave in a microwave safe bowl (covered with plastic wrap pierced a few times with a fork). Depending on how big the pieces are, this should take 2-4 minutes. Set aside. Heat a medium non-stick pan to medium heat. Add olive oil and wait until it's hot and shimmers. Add Italian cheese blend first, and form into a circle. Add the mozzarella cheese on top. Cook for 4-5 minutes until it gets crispy and you can easily slide a spatula under all the edges and can slide the crust onto a plate to cool. Set aside. Add mascarpone cheese, ghee, heavy cream, minced garlic, lemon pepper and salt to the hot pan, and cook for 5 minutes until bubbling. Stir frequently. Drizzle half the cream mixture over the crust, spreading it out as sauce. Add to the other half of the sauce in the pan. Cook for about 1 minute until hot and bubbling. Add the broccoli to the pizza, and serve hot.

Toasted Almond Tempeh

Yields: 1 serving
Per Serving: 316 calories
Net Carbs: 15.4 g
Total Fat: 18.1 g

Protein: 26.2 g
Macros: 13% C | 52% F | 33% P

Ingredients
2 tsp Almond butter
2 tsp Rice wine vinegar
1½ tsp Soy sauce
⅔ cup Tempeh
1 cup Broccoli (chopped)

Directions

Preheat oven (or toaster oven) to 350 F. Cover baking pan with aluminum foil and lightly coat with non-stick spray. Set aside. Combine almond butter, 1½ tsp vinegar, and 1 tsp soy sauce in a small bowl; set aside. Bring a small pot of water to boil with a steam tray placed over top. Once boiling add chopped broccoli to the steam tray and allow to cook for 4-5 minutes until bright green and tender. Remove from tray and set aside. Place sliced tempeh strips on prepared baking pan. Bake for 8 minutes, turn and bake for 5 more minutes, or until golden. Serve with almond sauce and steamed broccoli.

Spicy Egg Chutney

Yields: 4 servings

Per Serving: 246 calories

Net Carbs: 7.9 g

Total Fat: 16.7 g

Protein: 14.4 g

Macros: 16% C | 61% F | 23% P

Ingredients

8 large Eggs

1 medium Onion

Dash of Salt

1 cup Tomatoes (chopped or sliced)

3 Hot chili peppers

1 tsp Ginger (ground)

1 tsp Garlic powder

3 tsp Chili powder

Dash of Turmeric

2 tbsp Olive oil

Directions

Heat oil in pan and sauté the chopped onion. Add ground ginger, garlic, and turmeric. Once translucent, add the chili powder and stir to avoid sticking. Add the tomatoes and sliced peppers as well as salt to taste. Let it simmer for 2-3 minutes. Then crack the eggs into the mixture one by one. After a minute or two (when the eggs just begin to turn white), stir with a large spoon and stir well so the eggs scramble. Keep stirring slowly until the eggs are cooked and set. Serve warm.

Basil Tomato Pizza

Yields: 8 servings
Per Serving: 145 calories
Net Carbs: 4.6 g
Total Fat: 9 g
Protein: 10.2 g
Macros: 16% C | 56% F | 28% P

Ingredients

1 medium head Cauliflower
2 large Eggs
1½ cups Mozzarella cheese
2 tbsp Parmesan cheese (grated)
1 tbsp Italian seasoning
Dash of Salt
Dash of Pepper
1 spray Pam cooking spray
½ cup Pizza sauce
½ cup Cheddar cheese
12 Basil leaves (fresh, whole)
1 medium Plum tomato

Directions

Preheat oven to 425 F. Prepare a baking sheet with either parchment paper or a silicone baking mat. Add chopped cauliflower to a food processor and pulse until well-ground. Place ground cauliflower in a microwave-safe bowl. Cover loosely and microwave for 4-5 minutes, or until softened. Remove cover and let cool. Once cool, squeeze as much liquid out of the cauliflower as possible with a tea towel or cheesecloth. Place cauliflower in a large bowl and mix in the eggs, 1/2 cup mozzarella, parmesan cheese, Italian seasoning, and salt and pepper to taste. Smooth cauliflower mixture into an even rectangle onto the prepared baking sheet, approximately 15x10" in size. Spray lightly with nonstick spray and bake for 12-15 minutes, or until golden. Spoon pizza sauce onto the crust and top with cheese, sliced tomatoes, and basil leaves. Bake for another 3 to 5 minutes or until the cheese has melted. Serve immediately.

Sweet Potato Sesame Noodles

Yields: 2 servings
Per Serving: 335 calories
Net Carbs: 20.2 g
Total Fat: 25.3 g
Protein: 5 g
Macros: 24% C | 70% F | 6% P

Ingredients
1 Sweet potato (about 5" long)
1 tbsp Olive oil
2 tbsp Sesame butter
1 tbsp Sesame oil
2 tbsp Vinegar
2 tsp Honey
¼ tsp Red pepper flakes (crushed)
¼ tsp Salt
1 medium Scallion
1 tbsp Sesame seeds

Directions

Preheat oven to 425 F. Bake sweet potato for 10 minutes (it will not be fully cooked at this point). While the potato cools enough to handle, make the dressing: In a small bowl whisk together the tahini, sesame oil, vinegar, honey, red pepper flakes, and salt. Set aside. Spiralize the sweet potato into noodles. In a medium sauté pan, heat the olive oil and cook the sweet potato noodles for about 5 minutes. This will leave them slightly crunchy, but you can cook a bit more if you want them softer. Toss in the dressing, green onions, and sesame seeds. Serve warm or cold. Store in an airtight container in the fridge for up to one week.

VEGETABLES

Roasted Cashew Green Beans

Yields: 6 servings
Per Serving: 179 calories
Net Carbs: 11.2 g

Total Fat: 12.7 g
Protein: 4.8 g
Macros: 25% C | 64% F | 11% P

Ingredients
6 cups Green beans (chopped into ½" pieces)
8 tbsp Shallots (chopped)
2 tbsp Olive oil
¾ cup Cashews (whole or halves)

Directions
Preheat oven to 500 F with rack in lower 1/3 of oven. Roughly chop cashews. Toss green beans with cashews, shallots, oil, and salt and pepper to taste, then spread evenly in a large 4-sided sheet pan. Roast, stirring occasionally, until green beans are tender and nuts are golden brown, about 25 minutes. Season with salt and pepper.

Simple Sautéed Collard Greens

Total Fat: 2.8 g

Protein: 0.8 g

Macros: 34% C | 59% F | 7% P

Ingredients

1 tbsp Olive oil

1 cup Onions (chopped)

1 medium Tomato

1 cup Collard greens (chopped)

Yields: 5 servings

Per Serving: 43 calories

Net Carbs: 3.2 g

Directions

Heat a pan over medium-high heat. Dice onion and tomato, then sauté lightly in oil until onions are translucent. Add greens and stew together until greens are soft.

Spiced Eggplant & Peppers

Per Serving: 181 calories

Net Carbs: 7.5 g

Total Fat: 14.2 g

Protein: 2.3 g

Macros: 24% C | 71% F | 5% P

Yields: 4 servings

Ingredients

Dash of Salt

8 oz Eggplant

¼ tsp Saffron (optional)

1 cup Basil leaves (whole)

2 tbsp Red wine vinegar

¾ tsp Cumin (ground)

4 medium Red bell peppers

4 cloves Garlic

¼ cup Olive oil

¾ tsp Coriander seed

Directions

Remove stems and seeds from peppers and cut into 2" strips. Trim eggplant and quarter lengthwise. Cut into 2"-long pieces. Heat oil in a large skillet over medium-high heat. Add garlic, coriander, cumin, and saffron; cook, stirring often, until garlic is softened, about 4 minutes. Add sweet peppers and eggplant; season with salt and pepper. Cook, tossing occasionally, until vegetables are tender, 15-20 minutes. Remove from heat and add vinegar. Just before serving, add basil and toss to combine.

Cauliflower Rice

Per Serving: 93 calories
Net Carbs: 3.9 g
Total Fat: 7.1 g
Protein: 2.5 g
Macros: 20% C | 69% F | 11% P

Yields: 2 servings

Ingredients

1 small head Cauliflower
1 tbsp Olive oil
1 tsp Salt
Dash of Peppe

Directions

Cut cauliflower into large florets. Chop cauliflower into rice-sized pieces in food processor. Alternately, grate by hand on box grater. Heat oil in large frying pan over medium heat. Add cauliflower rice and sauté until just cooked through, about 5 minutes. Season with salt and pepper to taste.

Garlic Artichokes

Per Serving: 92 calories
Net Carbs: 4.9 g
Total Fat: 5.9 g
Protein: 2.9 g
Macros: 29% C | 58% F | 13% P

Ingredients

2 large Artichokes
3 cloves Garlic (minced)
2 tbsp Butter

Yields: 4 servings
Serving Size: ½ artichoke

Directions

Rinse artichokes under cold water, and use a sharp knife to cut the top 1/3 off of each. Trim the stems to about 1", and remove the smaller leaves from around the base. Use scissors to remove any remaining leaf tips. Cut each artichoke in half from the bottom to the top, then use a spoon to scrape out the hairy choke. Rinse again to remove any residual hairs. Melt the butter in a large skillet over medium heat. Add the garlic, and sauté for about 1 minute to flavor the butter. Arrange artichoke halves cut-side down in the skillet. Sauté for about 5 or 10 minutes, or until lightly browned. Reduce heat to low, and pour in about 1/4 cup of water, cover, and let steam for 15 to 20 minutes, or until the artichokes are tender. A fork should easily pierce the stem. Serve warm.

Bok Choy & Shallots

Total Fat: 23.7 g
Protein: 10.3 g
Macros: 13% C | 73% F | 14% P

Ingredients

8 tbsp Shallots (chopped)

8 heads Chinese cabbage (baby bok choy)

1¼ tsp Salt

2 cloves Garlic (minced)

1 cup Vegetable oil

Yields: 10 servings
Per Serving: 292 calories
Net Carbs: 9.2 g

Directions

Halve baby bok choy heads if larger, otherwise use whole. Heat a wok or 12-inch heavy skillet over moderate heat until a drop of water vaporizes instantly. Pour oil around side of wok, then tilt wok to swirl oil, coating side. When oil just begins to smoke, fry shallots in 3 batches, stirring, until golden brown, 3 to 5 minutes per batch. Transfer with a slotted spoon to paper towels to drain. Toss fried shallots with 1/4 teaspoon salt (shallots will crisp as they cool). Pour off all but 3 tbsp oil from wok, then add garlic, bok choy, and remaining 1 tsp salt to wok and cook over moderate heat, covered, stirring occasionally, until crisp-tender, about 5 minutes. Serve topped with fried shallots.

Garlic Spinach

Yields: 4 servings
Per Serving: 72 calories
Net Carbs: 3.9 g

Total Fat: 3.9 g
Protein: 4.5 g
Macros: 26% C | 49% F | 25% P

Ingredients

1 tbsp Olive oil

6 cloves Garlic (minced)

2 packages (10 oz each) Spinach (raw)

1 tsp Garlic powder

½ tsp Lemon juice

Directions

Add olive oil to skillet over medium heat. Stir in garlic; cook and stir until fragrant, about 2 minutes. Add the spinach a few handfuls at a time, stirring until wilted before adding more, about 5 minutes. Stir in the lemon juice, and season with garlic salt.

BREAKFASTS

Spinach Scramble

Total Fat: 10.6 g

Protein: 7 g

Macros: 8% C | 71% F | 21% P

Ingredients

½ cup Spinach (raw)

2 tbsp Onions (chopped)

1 large Egg

Dash of Salt

Dash of Pepper

½ tbsp Butter

Yields: 1 serving

Per Serving: 134 calories

Net Carbs: 2.1 g

Directions

Heat sauté pan on medium/low heat. Melt butter. Add onions and sauté in pan until translucent. Add spinach and eggs. Gently stir and scramble eggs, add salt and pepper. Remove from heat.

Keto Pancakes

Yields: 2 servings

Serving Size: 4 mini-pancakes

Per Serving: 651 calories

Net Carbs: 4.8 g

Total Fat: 59.6 g

Protein: 21.1 g

Macros: 5% C | 82% F | 13% P

Ingredients
4 extra large Eggs

½ cup Almond flour

½ tsp Baking soda

2 tsp Stevia

1 tsp Cream of tartar

5 tbsp Coconut oil

2 tsp Vanilla extract

Directions
Crack eggs in a bowl and beat. In a separate bowl, combine almond flour, baking soda, stevia, and cream of tartar until well combined. Add the vanilla extract and 4 tbsp melted coconut oil to the eggs. Add the dry ingredients to the egg mixture. Mix until well combined. Grease the pan with remaining coconut oil and create 4 small pancakes for every serving. Cook on low heat for 5 minutes until the top of the pancake begins to firm up. Flip and cook the other side for 1 minute. Remove from heat and serve warm.

Green Eggs

Yields: 1 serving

Per Serving: 222 calories

Net Carbs: 3.2 g

Total Fat: 15.6 g

Protein: 16.3 g

Macros: 8% C | 63% F | 29% P

Ingredients

2 extra large Eggs

½ cup Spinach (raw)

½ cup Kale (raw, chopped)

½ cup Chard (raw, chopped)

1 tsp Coconut oil

Directions

Mix eggs and greens in a food processor until smooth. Melt coconut oil in a skillet over medium heat. Pour egg mixture into pan and cook. Scramble eggs to desired doneness and serve immediately.

Ket-Oats

Yields: 1 serving

Per Serving: 240 calories

Net Carbs: 9 g

Total Fat: 13.7 g

Protein: 7.7 g

Macros: 36% C | 51% F | 13% P

Ingredients

2 tbsp Chia seeds

2 tbsp Flaxseed (ground)

½ cup Almond milk

⅛ tsp Stevia extract

¼ cup Strawberries (sliced)

Directions

Combine all ingredients except strawberries in a pot on the stove over medium heat. Bring to a boil, stirring frequently. Remove from heat at desired consistency. Add sliced strawberries and serve hot.

Veggie-Egg Skillet

Yields: 3 servings
Per Serving: 327 calories
Net Carbs: 5.3 g
Total Fat: 25.7 g
Protein: 16.9 g
Macros: 8% C | 71% F | 21% P

Ingredients

⅔ cup plain Greek yogurt
1 clove Garlic
1 tbsp Butter
2 tbsp Olive oil
3 tbsp Leeks (chopped)
2 tbsp Scallions (chopped)
10 cups Spinach (raw)
1 tsp Lemon juice
4 extra large Eggs
¼ tsp Chili powder
1 tsp Oregano

Directions

Mix yogurt, garlic clove, and a pinch of salt in a small bowl. Set aside. Preheat oven to 300 F. Melt 1 tbsp butter with oil in a large heavy skillet over medium heat. Add leek (chopped) and scallion (white and pale green parts, chopped); reduce heat to low. Cook until soft, about 10 minutes. Add spinach and lemon juice; season with salt to taste. Increase heat to medium-high; cook, turning frequently, until wilted, 4–

5 minutes. Transfer spinach mixture to 10" oven-safe skillet, leaving any excess liquid behind. If using 2 smaller skillets, divide spinach mixture equally between skillets. Make 4 deep indentations in center of spinach in larger skillet or 2 indentations in each small skillet. Carefully break 1 egg into each hollow, taking care to keep yolks intact. Bake until egg whites are set, 10–15 minutes. Serve warm.

Smoky Scramble

Yields: 4 servings
Per Serving: 264 calories
Net Carbs: 4.6 g
Total Fat: 20.7 g
Protein: 13.7 g
Macros: 8% C | 71% F | 21% P

Ingredients

3 extra large Eggs
Dash of Salt
Dash of Pepper
8 oz Mushrooms (sliced)
1 medium Green bell pepper
1 tsp Garlic (minced)
1 tbsp Smoked paprika
1 tbsp Hot sauce
1 cup Cheddar cheese (shredded)
2 tbsp Olive oil

Directions

Whisk eggs. Combine with salt and pepper to taste. Over medium-high heat, sauté the mushrooms in 1 tbsp olive oil until cooked down, about 5 minutes. Remove and set aside Add another 1 tbsp olive oil to the pan and sauté bell peppers and garlic for 2 minutes. Reduce heat to medium and add eggs to the pan and stir to combine. Add mushrooms back into the pan. Stir to mix. Season with smoked paprika and hot sauce. Continue stirring until the eggs are fully cooked, about 5 minutes. Remove from heat and fold in cheddar cheese. Serve hot.

Green & White Omelet

Yields: 1 omelet
Per Serving: 164 calories
Net Carbs: 6.1 g
Total Fat: 9.6 g

Protein: 11.7 g
Macros: 18% C | 53% F | 29% P

<u>Ingredients</u>
3 large Egg whites
¼ cup Onions (chopped)
¼ cup Green bell pepper
2 tsp Coconut oil
2 tbsp Almond milk

<u>Directions</u>
Lightly sauté pepper and onions in coconut oil, then remove vegetables from the pan and set aside. Whisk egg white until fluffy, then add almond milk. Add egg mixture to skillet, and cook until bottom firms slightly. Add vegetables. When partly cooked, fold egg over vegetables twice and roll into an omelet. Cook until eggs are cooked through. Serve warm.

Spicy Sweet Potato Hash with Eggs

Per Serving: 322 calories
Net Carbs: 17.5 g
Total Fat: 20.2 g
Protein: 14.3 g
Macros: 26% C | 56% F | 18% P

Yields: 3 servings

Ingredients
2 Sweet potatoes (about 5" long)
3 cloves Garlic (minced)
2 Serrano peppers
½ cup Onions (chopped)
2 tbsp Olive oil
6 large Eggs

Directions
Begin by cutting sweet potatoes into 1/2" cubes. Trim garlic and mince garlic and peppers. Chop onion. In a large cast-iron skillet, add olive oil and warm it over medium-high. When the oil is glistening, add the garlic, onion, and serrano pepper. Add sweet potatoes and toss to coat. Increase the heat back to medium-high and cook the potatoes until they are tender, about 25 minutes. Meanwhile, in a separate pan coated with non-stick spray, cook eggs until yolk has reached desired doneness. When the potatoes have fully cooked, serve topped with eggs.

Blueberry-Almond Butter Waffles

Per Serving: 464 calories
Net Carbs: 14.4 g
Total Fat: 37.1 g
Protein: 17.6 g
Macros: 13% C | 72% F | 15% P

Yields: 3 servings

Ingredients

2/3 cup Almond butter

2 extra large Eggs

½ medium Banana

¼ tsp Vanilla extract

½ tbsp Coconut oil

⅓ cup Almond milk (unsweetened)

1 tbsp Sunflower seed flour

½ tsp Baking soda

1 tsp Cinnamon

⅛ tsp Salt

⅔ cup Blueberries

Directions

Preheat waffle iron and spray with nonstick cooking spray. In a large bowl, whisk together almond butter, eggs, banana, vanilla extract, coconut oil, and almond milk until well combined and there aren't any large lumps. Stir in flour, baking soda, cinnamon, and salt; mix until well combined. Gently fold in blueberries. Spoon batter into waffle iron and cook until steaming stops and waffles are golden brown and slightly crispy on the outside. Repeat with remaining batter. Serve hot.

Green Pea Mini-Frittatas

Macros: 11% C | 66% F | 23% P

<u>Ingredients</u>
2 tbsp Olive oil
½ cup Peas (whole)
1 Leek
6 extra large Eggs
Dash of Salt
2 oz Ricotta cheese
⅛ cup Peppermint (fresh)
Dash of Pepper

Yields: 6 servings
Per Serving: 145 calories
Net Carbs: 3.1 g
Total Fat: 10.6 g
Protein: 8.5 g

<u>Directions</u>
Blanch peas in boiling water for approximately 3-4 minutes, then place immediately in an ice bath. Slice leeks into thin strips. Tear mint leaves into small pieces to release flavor. Preheat oven to 425 F. Heat the oil in a large ovenproof sauté pan over medium heat. Add the leek and sauté until soft, then add the peas and cook for 2 to 3 minutes more. Meanwhile, in a medium bowl, beat the eggs with 1 tbsp water. Add the eggs and half the mint to the pan, season with the salt and pepper, and cook, lifting the edges with a spatula to allow the uncooked eggs to flow to the bottom. When the frittata is partly cooked (7-10 minutes),

sprinkle on the ricotta, and transfer the pan to the oven. Bake until puffed, golden, and set, 8-10 minutes. Remove and allow to cool slightly. Garnish with the remaining mint to taste and serve.

Savory Waffles

Yields: 6 servings
Serving Size: 1 waffle
Per Serving: 111 calories
Net Carbs: 2 g
Total Fat: 7.4 g
Protein: 8.8 g
Macros: 8% C | 60% F | 32% P

Ingredients

1 cup Cauliflower (chopped)
1 cup Mozzarella cheese (shredded)
⅓ cup Parmesan cheese (grated)
2 medium Eggs
1 tsp Garlic powder
1 tsp Onion powder
½ tsp Pepper
1 tbsp Chives (chopped)
¼ tbsp Parsley (fresh)
1 piece (3 g) Sun-dried tomatoes

Directions

Heat waffle maker. Chop cauliflower in food processor until "riced". Combine with other ingredients and mix well to make batter. Add scant ¼ cup of batter to griddle. Set timer for 4-6 minutes, checking after 4 minutes. If waffle is sticking, allow to cook for slightly longer. Remove from waffle maker once cooked through, and repeat with the remaining batter. Allow to cool slightly before serving.

Veggie Egg Muffins

Yields: 12 servings
Serving Size: 1 muffin
Per Serving: 113 calories
Net Carbs: 2.2 g
Total Fat: 7.2 g

Protein: 8.6 g
Macros: 13% C | 57% F | 30% P

Ingredients
12 large Eggs
1½ cups Carrots (grated)
½ cup Red bell pepper (chopped)
½ cup Peas
1 cup Spinach (raw)
½ cup Mushrooms (pieces and stems, chopped)
Dash of Salt
Dash of Pepper
¾ cup Cheddar cheese (shredded)

Directions

Preheat oven to 375 F. Spray non-stick 12-cup muffin pan with cooking spray. In a large bowl, add carrots, peppers, peas, spinach, and mushrooms. Toss to combine. Loosely pile about 3 tbsp of vegetable mixture to each muffin cup, about ⅔ to ¾ full. Crack eggs into a 2-cup glass measuring cup, and lightly beat with a whisk. Add salt and pepper to taste, and whisk to combine. Pour about 2-3 tbsp of egg into each muffin cup – about ¾ full. Top each muffin cup with about 1 tbsp cheese. Bake for 18-20 minutes, or until muffins are set, cooked through, and golden. Allow muffins to cool in the pan on a wire rack for 10 minutes before removing from pan. Serve warm.

Blueberry Chia Breakfast Pudding

Protein: 9.2 g

Macros: 20% C | 71% F | 9% P

Ingredients

1 cup Coconut milk

1 cup plain Kefir (lowfat)

3 Avocado

1 cup Blueberries

4 tbsp Chia seeds

½ tsp Salt

1 tbsp Vanilla extract

1 tbsp Honey

Yields: 4 servings

Per Serving: 426 calories

Net Carbs: 9.9 g

Total Fat: 33.4 g

Directions

Remove avocado pits and skins, and place in blender with other ingredients. Blend all ingredients together in a high-powered blender. Refrigerate and serve cold.

Jalapeno Breakfast Muffins

Serving Size: 1 muffin
Per Serving: 198 calories
Net Carbs: 1 g
Total Fat: 16.7 g
Protein: 10.7 g
Macros: 2% C | 76% F | 22% P

Yields: 12 servings

Ingredients

9 extra large Eggs

¾ cup Heavy whipping cream

9 oz Cheddar cheese

Dash of Salt

Dash of Pepper

¼ cup Jalapeno pepper (sliced)

Directions

Preheat oven to 350 F. Mix eggs, cream, cheese, salt, and pepper in a bowl, and whisk. Evenly distribute into 12 muffin cups. Add a few chopped or sliced jalapenos to each muffin. Bake for at least 15-20 minutes, until muffins are cooked through. Serve warm.

Creamy Goat Cheese Scrambled Eggs & Asparagus

Ingredients

1 lb Asparagus

¼ cup Water

1 Lemon

1 tbsp Chives (chopped)

8 large Eggs

4 oz Goat cheese (soft)

½ tsp Salt

Dash of Pepper

2 tbsp Butter

Yields: 4 servings

Per Serving: 298 calories

Net Carbs: 4.1 g

Total Fat: 21.4 g

Protein: 20.6 g

Macros: 7% C | 65% F | 28% P

Directions

Wash and dry asparagus. Remove the tough lower part of the asparagus (usually 1-2"). In a dry skillet over medium-high heat, cook the asparagus, stirring occasionally. After 3 minutes, add about ¼ cup water and cook for another 3-4 minutes. Taste a piece, and continue to cook until the thickest pieces are tender, adding additional water if necessary. Sprinkle with kosher salt. If desired, garnish with lemon zest or lemon juice. Wash and chop chives. In a medium bowl, crack 8 eggs and whisk them together until well-beaten. Crumble the goat cheese and stir it into the eggs, along with ½ tsp kosher salt and plenty of fresh ground pepper. In a skillet, heat 2 tbsp butter over medium heat. Tilt the pan to ensure the entire pan is coated in the melted butter. Pour in the eggs. Keep the heat on medium. When the eggs just start to set, use a flat spatula to slowly scrape sections of eggs, creating folds. Scrape occasionally until the eggs form soft folds, and remove them from the heat just before they are fully hardened. Serve immediately, garnished with chopped chives (if desired) and alongside asparagus spears.

Easy Poached Eggs

Yields: 1 serving
Per Serving: 72 calories
Net Carbs: 0.4 g
Total Fat: 4.8 g
Protein: 6.3 g
Macros: 5% C | 60% F | 35% P

Ingredients

1 large Egg
⅛ tsp Vinegar
⅓ cup Water

Directions

Add the water and white vinegar to a 6-ounce custard cup. Break egg into cup, pierce egg yolk with toothpick, and cover dish loosely with plastic wrap. Place in microwave and cook for about 1 minute or until cooked to desired doneness. Immediately remove egg from hot water with a slotted spoon (or it will continue to cook). Serve with salt and pepper to taste.

Low-Carb Breakfast Porridge

⅛ cup Hemp seeds (shelled)

¼ cup Walnuts (pieces)

¼ cup Coconut meat

2 tbsp Chia seeds

¾ cup Almond milk (unsweetened)

¼ cup Coconut milk (canned, unsweetened)

¼ cup Almond butter

1 tbsp Coconut oil

½ tsp Turmeric

1 tsp Cinnamon

Dash of Pepper

Yields: 4 servings

Per Serving: 292 calories

Net Carbs: 6.7 g

Total Fat: 25.6 g

Protein: 7.4 g

Macros: 11% C | 79% F | 10% P

Ingredients

Directions

Roughly chop the walnuts. Place the hemp seeds, chopped walnuts, and flaked coconut into a hot pan and roast for 1-2 minutes or until fragrant. Toss a few times to prevent burning. When done, transfer the roasted mix into a bowl and set aside. In a small saucepan, mix coconut milk and almond milk and heat over a medium heat. Once hot (not boiling), remove from heat. Add almond butter, coconut oil, chia seeds, turmeric powder, cinnamon, and black pepper. Mix until well combined and set aside for 5-10 minutes. Stir in half of the roasted mix. Spoon the porridge into serving bowls and top with remaining roasted mix. Serve immediately or store in the fridge for up to 3 days.

Cheddar Broccoli Quiche

Macros: 21% C | 66% F | 13% P

Ingredients

½ cup Cheddar cheese (shredded)
Dash of Pepper
½ cup Broccoli
3 extra large Eggs
1 Pie crust (9")
1½ cups Half and half

Yields: 8 servings
Per Serving: 202 calories
Net Carbs: 10.2 g
Total Fat: 14.8 g
Protein: 6.7 g

Directions

Preheat oven to 375 F. Prick the bottom of a 9" pie shell and bake for approximately 10 minutes. Remove from oven. In pie shell, layer half of the cheddar cheese, broccoli, and the other half of the cheese. Sprinkle with pepper. Combine eggs and half and half and pour over eggs and broccoli. Bake until golden brown, until a silver knife inserted 1" from the edge of crust comes out clean. Serve warm.

Pumpkin Spice Waffles

Yields: 2 servings
Serving Size: 2 waffles
Per Serving: 275 calories
Net Carbs: 7.3 g
Total Fat: 19.3 g
Protein: 13.4 g
Macros: 18% C | 63% F | 19% P

Ingredients

⅓ cup Coconut milk (unsweetened)
¼ cup Pumpkin (canned)
2 extra large Eggs
1 tsp Vanilla extract
⅓ cup Almond flour
2 tbsp Flaxseed (ground)
½ tbsp Pumpkin pie spice
1 tsp Baking powder
¼ oz Stevia (or similar sweetener)

Directions

Mix all wet ingredients together, then sift dry ingredients into wet ingredients. Mix everything together until a slightly liquid batter is formed. Heat waffle iron, then spray with coconut oil, then pour batter onto waffle iron. Cook until waffle iron indicates it is finished, then cook longer (if you prefer it crispier) or remove waffles. Top with desired toppings, and serve warm.

Cashew-Asparagus Omelet

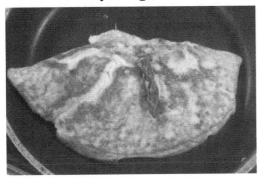

Yields: 4 servings

Serving Size: 1 omelet

Per Serving: 330 calories

Net Carbs: 6.4 g

Total Fat: 23.8 g

Protein: 22.1 g

Macros: 8% C | 65% F | 27% P

Ingredients

2 oz Cashews

6 extra large Eggs

2 tbsp Water

1 cup Parmesan cheese (shredded)

1 tbsp Parsley

Dash of Salt

Dash of Pepper

1 tsp Olive oil

1 tbsp Butter

8 oz Asparagus

Directions

Roast cashews for a few minutes in a dry frying pan over medium heat to release flavor. In a bowl, beat eggs with roasted cashews, water, cheese, and parsley. Season with salt and pepper to taste. Warm the same pan over medium heat. Add oil and butter. When the butter melts, pour in the egg mixture and cook, letting it sit until it is softly set but still moist. Add the asparagus tips and cook 4-5 minutes longer. Serve immediately.

DESERTS

Chia Coconut Bars

Yields: 6 servings
Per Serving: 175 calories
Net Carbs: 5.9 g
Total Fat: 14.2 g
Protein: 3.9 g

Macros: 19% C | 73% F | 9% P

Ingredients
4 tbsp Chia seeds
1 cup Water
1 cup Coconut (shredded, unsweetened)
1 tbsp Coconut oil
1 tbsp Powdered sugar (unsifted)
¼ tsp Vanilla extract
½ cup Cashews

Directions
Soak the chia seeds in water for about 15 minutes, until they become gelatinous. Preheat oven to 350 F. Mix the soaked chia seeds with the shredded coconut, coconut oil, powdered sugar, and vanilla extract, until all ingredients are well blended. Add cashews and mix well. Line a 9" x 9" baking pan with parchment paper. Place the chia coconut mix on the parchment paper and flatten it with your hands until it fills the whole pan (it should be about ¾" thick). Bake for 45 minutes or until golden on the edges and dry in the middle. You can insert a toothpick in

the middle to check dryness. Let cool in the pan, then remove and cut into 6 bars.

Chocolate Tofu Mousse

Total Fat: 13.7 g
Protein: 64.8 g
Macros: 10% C | 29% F | 61% P

Ingredients
16 oz Tofu (soft)
3 tbsp Cocoa powder
1 tbsp Maple syrup
4 scoops (60 g) Protein powder

Yields: 2 servings
Per Serving: 426 calories
Net Carbs: 14.1 g

Directions
Combine all ingredients in a blender and pulse until smooth. Serve cold.

PB-Chia Protein Balls

Yields: 10 servings
Serving Size: 1 protein ball
Per Serving: 88 calories
Net Carbs: 7.9 g
Total Fat: 4.2 g
Protein: 3.9 g
Macros: 39% C | 43% F | 18% P

Ingredients

1 scoop (30 g) Protein powder

4 Medjool dates (pitted)

4 tbsp Peanut butter

1 oz Chia seeds

Directions

Pulse all ingredients together in a food processor. Roll into 10 tablespoon-sized balls. Serve, and store extra in refrigerator.

Lemon-Coconut Mousse

Yields: 4 servings

Per Serving: 250 calories

Net Carbs: 9.8 g

Total Fat: 24.1 g

Protein: 2.3 g

Macros: 9% C | 87% F | 4% P

Ingredients

2 cups Coconut milk (canned, unsweetened)

2 tbsp Sugar

½ tsp Vanilla extract

Zest of 1 lemon

Dash of Salt

Directions

For the coconut cream, refrigerate two cans of coconut milk overnight (several days if possible) then scoop out the cream that rises to the top and reserve the liquid for other uses. In a small bowl zest one lemon and combine zest with sugar, rubbing the mixture between your fingers to help infuse the sugar with the lemon flavor. In a large bowl of a heavy-duty mixer or with an electric hand mixer, fitted with whisk attachment, beat/whip coconut cream and salt, starting on low, increasing incrementally to medium speed until soft peaks become visible, about 2 minutes. Add the sugar mixture and vanilla extract and beat until the mixture is smooth and the sugar is no longer visible. Divide the mixture evenly among ramekins and refrigerate until ready to serve.

Ginger Grapefruit Chia Pudding

Yields: 2 servings
Per Serving: 480 calories
Net Carbs: 10.1 g
Total Fat: 31.9 g

Protein: 12 g
Macros: 20% C | 60% F | 10% P

Ingredients
½ cup Coconut milk
1½ cups Almond milk
6 tbsp Chia seeds
1 tsp Ginger root
1 medium Grapefruit
1 tsp Vanilla extract
¼ cup Coconut (flaked)
2 tsp Maple syrup

Directions
In a large bowl, whisk together the canned coconut milk, almond milk, chia seeds, ginger, vanilla, and maple syrup. Cover and refrigerate for at

least 2 hours to thicken, whisking or shaking occasionally (can leave overnight). Spoon the pudding into individual servings, top with grapefruit slices and coconut, and serve cold.

Coconut Avocado Truffles

Yields: 12 servings
Serving Size: 1 truffle
Per Serving: 200 calories
Net Carbs: 9.7 g

Total Fat: 15.2 g
Protein: 2.4 g
Macros: 27% C | 68% F | 5% P

<u>Ingredients</u>
2 Avocado
1½ cups Dark chocolate chips
1 tsp Vanilla extract
Dash of Salt
½ cup Coconut (shredded)

<u>Directions</u>
Remove avocado from the skins and remove the pits. Place the avocado in a food processor and pulse until the avocado is completely smooth. Set aside. Add the chocolate chips to a large microwave safe bowl and melt at 50% power for 1 minute. Stir well. If they're not completely melted, continue to melt the chocolate chips at 50% power for 15 seconds, stirring after each heating. When the chocolate is melted, stir in the avocado, vanilla extract, and salt. Mix until completely combined, then refrigerate for 2 hours or overnight. When the mixture is chilled,

use a tablespoon to scoop and then roll into round truffles, then immediately roll the truffles in coconut. Store truffles in an airtight container in the refrigerator up to 2 weeks.

PB-Chocolate Banana Bites

Net Carbs: 10.5 g
Total Fat: 7.8 g
Protein: 2.7 g
Macros: 36% C | 56% F | 9% P

Ingredients
1 medium Banana
⅓ cup Peanut butter
4 oz Dark chocolate

Yields: 12 servings
Serving Size: 3 bites
Per Serving: 126 calories

Directions
Slice bananas into slices about ¼-½" thick. Spread a little nut butter onto each slice, and sandwich two slices together. Place on wax paper on a cookie sheet and freeze until solid, at least an hour. Melt chocolate in a double boiler and remove frozen banana bites from freezer. Dip each banana bite in chocolate and place back on wax paper. Freeze for another hour. Serve cold.

Chai-Chia Pudding

Yields: 1 serving
Per Serving: 358 calories
Net Carbs: 0 g
Total Fat: 21.9 g
Protein: 12.1 g
Macros: 31% C | 55% F | 14% P

Ingredients

1 cup Almond milk (unsweetened)

3 tbsp Chia seeds

2 tsp Vanilla extract

½ tsp Cinnamon

½ tsp Ginger

¼ tsp Cardamom (ground)

¼ tsp Cloves

1 tbsp Flaxseed (whole)

Directions

Stir all ingredients together. Refrigerate for 2 hours or overnight. Serve cold.

Keto Coconut Peppermint Patties

Protein: 0.5 g
Macros: 1% C | 98% F | 1% P

Ingredients
¼ cup Coconut cream
¼ cup Coconut (unsweetened, shredded)
3 tbsp Coconut oil
½ tsp Peppermint (fresh, finely chopped)
1½ tsp Mocha powder

Yields: 8 servings
Serving Size: 3 patties
Per Serving: 81 calories
Net Carbs: 1.3 g
Total Fat: 8.8 g

Directions
Mix together melted coconut cream, shredded coconut, 1 tbsp coconut oil, and finely chopped peppermint. Pour coconut butter mixture into mini-muffin tins (fill each cup halfway). Place in refrigerator and allow to harden for about 15 minutes. Mix together remaining 2 tbsp coconut oil and cocoa powder. Remove muffin tin from refrigerator, and top each tin with cocoa mixture. Return to refrigerator until the chocolate has set. Thaw for about 5 minutes prior to serving.

Tropical Avocado Popsicles

Yields: 6 servings
Serving Size: 1 popsicle
Per Serving: 249 calories

Net Carbs: 4.3 g
Total Fat: 24.1 g
Protein: 2.7 g
Macros: 9% C | 87% F | 4% P

Ingredients

2 Avocado
1½ cups Coconut milk
4 packets Splenda
2 tbsp Lime juice

Directions

Place all ingredients into a blender; secure lid and pulse to break down ingredients. Scrape down the inner sides of the blender to incorporate splattered ingredients and replace lid. Blend until the mixture is a smooth, creamy consistency without lumps. Taste and adjust sweetener to your liking, using less or more. Evenly distribute the mixture into 6 popsicle molds. The blended ingredients are thick; you may find spooning the mixture into the molds easier than pouring. Tap the filled molds on the counter top to remove air bubbles and settle the mixture. Place popsicle sticks or handles into the mixture in the center of the molds. Freeze the molds for several hours, until the mixture has completely solidified. When you are ready to eat, run the mold under water briefly to help release the popsicle. Gently pull the popsicle out by the handle, and serve frozen.

Avocado-Chocolate Protein Mousse

Protein: 4.6 g

Macros: 9% C | 76% F | 15% P

Ingredients

1 Avocado

1 packet Stevia

½ scoop (15 g) Protein powder

2 tbsp Coconut cream

⅓ cup Water

Yields: 3 servings

Per Serving: 125 calories

Net Carbs: 1.6 g

Total Fat: 10.6 g

Directions

Combine all ingredients in a blender and pulse until smooth. Serve cold.

Protein Fluff

Per Serving: 113 calories

Net Carbs: 4.9 g

Total Fat: 3.4 g

Protein: 15.2 g

Macros: 19% C | 27% F | 54% P

Ingredients

3 cups Cottage cheese

1 package Gelatin

1 cup Whipped cream

Yields: 6 servings

of skillet. Pour berries on top. Bake for 28-30 minutes, or until cake is firm in center and lightly golden.

Lemon Fat Bombs

Protein: 0.2 g
Macros: 1% C | 98% F | 1% P

Ingredients
2 oz Cream cheese
4 tbsp Butter
4 tbsp Coconut oil
2 packets Splenda
Juice of 3 wedges lemon
4 tbsp Heavy whipping cream

Yields: 16 servings
Serving Size: 1 fat bomb
Per Serving: 81 calories
Net Carbs: 0.3 g
Total Fat: 8.8 g

Directions

Melt the cream cheese in the microwave in short bursts. Then, add the butter and coconut oil and melt some more. Whisk together and then add the sweetener, lemon juice, and whipping cream. Whisk and then pour into silicone molds. Freeze to set, then store in the refrigerator. Serve cold.

Raw Chocolate Macaroons

Yields: 32 servings

Serving Size: 1 macaroon

Per Serving: 64 calories

Net Carbs: 4.6 g

Total Fat: 5 g

Protein: 0.3 g

Macros: 28% C | 70% F | 2% P

Ingredients

2 cups Coconut (unsweetened)

½ cup Coconut oil

5 tbsp Cocoa powder (unsweetened)

¼ cup Honey

½ tsp Vanilla extract

¼ tsp Salt

Directions

Place all ingredients into a food processor and process until well mixed, scraping down the sides as needed. Make sure that all ingredients are incorporated; it will be thick. Roll into little balls with your hands, or scoop some dough out, and plop down on a wax paper. Chill in the freezer or fridge. Store in an airtight container in the fridge or freezer. Serve cold.

Chocolate Chip Cookie Dough Protein Balls

Yields: 22 servings
Serving Size: 2 protein balls
Per Serving: 162 calories
Net Carbs: 8.5 g
Total Fat: 10.7 g
Protein: 6.6 g
Macros: 25% C | 59% F | 16% P

Ingredients

2 cups Peanuts (dry-roasted, unsalted)

3 scoops (90 g) Protein powder

¼ cup Coconut (unsweetened, shredded)

1 tbsp Vanilla extract

3 tbsp Almond butter

1 cup Dates (chopped)

¼ cup Water

2 oz Cacao nibs

Directions

Add 2 cups of dry roasted peanuts to your food processor and blend until it is peanut flour. Add your protein powder and pulse until blended. Add your unsweetened coconut and pulse until blended. Add the vanilla extract, almond butter, dates, and water. Blend until cookie dough texture. Begin rolling protein balls into 1" balls. Press in cacao nibs. Refrigerate up to a week. Serve cold.

Low-Carb Coconut Crisps

Per Serving: 31 calories
Net Carbs: 2.5 g
Total Fat: 2.2 g
Protein: 0.2 g
Macros: 23% C | 64% F | 3% P

Yields: 16 servings

Ingredients

2 sheets Phyllo dough
2 tsp Sugar
⅓ cup Coconut meat (unsweetened)
1 tbsp Butter
1 tbsp Vegetable oil

Directions

Melt butter. Thaw phyllo if frozen, cover with 2 overlapping pieces of plastic wrap and then a damp kitchen towel. Preheat oven to 400 F. Stir together butter and oil. Arrange 1 phyllo sheet on a work surface with a long side of phyllo nearest you, keeping remaining sheet covered. Brush with some butter mixture and sprinkle with 1 tsp sugar. Top with remaining sheet of phyllo, then brush with remaining butter mixture and sprinkle with remaining 1 tsp sugar. Cut phyllo in half crosswise and stack. Cut stack into quarters and cut each quarter diagonally twice (in an X) to form 4 triangles (for a total of 16 triangles). Arrange triangles, spaced evenly, on 2 ungreased baking sheets and sprinkle with coconut. Bake in middle and lower third of oven, switching position of sheets halfway through baking, until golden and crisp, 5-6 minutes total. Serve warm.

Chapter 9:

2-Week Vegetarian Keto Meal Plan

Note: This meal plan is based on an approximately 1800 to 2000-calorie diet. If you require more or less than this, you may need to make some slight adjustments to the plan. We aim for approximately 70% of calories from fat, 20% from protein, and 10% from carbohydrates (approximately 45 grams net carbohydrates or less), but these macros will vary slightly from day to day.

Remember when we discussed macros and net carbs? Here's what you need to know about this meal plan: the number of net carbs are listed after the meal plan for each day, but the macros are calculated based on total carbs (since they wouldn't otherwise add up to 100%).

As this is a vegetarian keto plan, it contains quite a bit of eggs and cheese (in order to meet your protein and fat goals without meat). If you do not consume eggs or dairy, you will need to locate suitable substitutions for those meals.

Make sure to check the serving size for each recipe – most are for 1 serving only, while others may be for several servings. The shopping list contains items only, not quantities. If you intend to cook for more than 1 person or meal prep in advance for multiple servings, you may need to adjust your ingredients and shopping list accordingly.

All recipes follow the meal plan, as well as a grocery list. Bon Appetit!

Meal Plan

Week 1 - Day 1

Breakfast - Keto Lemon Blueberry Muffin

Lunch - Spinach & Cheese Omelet, Keto Mushroom Chips

Dinner - 5 Minute Keto Pizza, Spinach Salad with Blackberries

Snack – Keto Protein Shake

Snack – Dark Chocolate Raspberry Fat Bombs

1811 calories

Net Carbs: 28.9 g

Total Fat: 139.6 g

Protein: 93.1 g

Macros: 11% C | 69% F | 20% P

Week 1 - Day 2

Breakfast – Bulletproof Coffee, Coconut Flour Waffles

Lunch – Herbed Lemon Tofu, Roasted Cauliflower & Tahini

Dinner – Mediterranean Omelet with Fennel, Olives, & Dill, Grilled Asparagus

Snack – Cheese Cubes

Snack – Strawberry Cheesecake Fat Bombs

1907 calories

Net Carbs: 27.4 g

Total Fat: 163.6 g

Protein: 75.6 g

Macros: 8% C | 77% F | 15% P

Week 1 – Day 3

Breakfast – Cream Cheese Pancakes

Lunch – Avocado Egg Bake, Cloud Bread

Dinner – Tomato & Basil Salad, Baked Spinach Chips

Snack – Strawberries

Snack – Mint Fudge Fat Bombs

1849 calories

Net Carbs: 38.7 g

Total Fat: 152 g

Protein: 69.9 g

Macros: 14% C | 74% F | 12% P

Week 1 – Day 4

Breakfast – Keto Pumpkin Protein Bar

Lunch – Low-Carb Asiago Baked Eggs, Kale Chips

Dinner – Caramelized Cauliflower Steaks, Quick & Easy Low-Carb Caprese Salad

Snack – Keto Protein Shake

Snack – Chocolate Fat Bombs

1933 calories

Net Carbs: 35 g

Total Fat: 157.7 g

Protein: 97.8 g

Macros: 11% C | 73% F | 16% P

Week 1 – Day 5

Breakfast – Iced Coffee Protein Shake, Greek Yogurt with Blueberries, Walnuts, & Honey

Lunch – Cucumber Avocado Salad, Low-Carb Jalapeno Cheese Crisps

Dinner – Asparagus, Fontina and Tomato Frittata

Snack – Pecans (1 oz)

Snack – Grilled Peaches with Honey

1844 calories

Net Carbs: 47.4 g

Total Fat: 138.9 g

Protein: 94.6 g

Macros: 15% C | 68% F | 17% P

Week 1 – Day 6

Breakfast – Avocado Egg Stack

Lunch – Low-Carb Spicy Nachos

Dinner – Zucchini Alfredo

Snack – Chia Cottage Cheese with Blueberries

Snack – Mint Fudge Fat Bombs

1959 calories

Net Carbs: 32.9 g

Total Fat: 164.9 g

Protein: 74.3 g

Macros: 13% C | 76% F | 11% P

Week 1 – Day 7

Breakfast – Spinach Avocado Smoothie Bowl

Lunch – Cauliflower-Crusted Grilled Cheese Sandwich

Dinner – Parmesan & Mushroom Baked Eggs, Easy Sautéed Eggplant

Snack – Strawberry Cheesecake Fat Bombs

Snack – Protein-Boosted Yogurt

1831 calories

Macros: 10% C | 70% F | 20% P

Net Carbs: 30.5 g   *Total Fat: 142.2 g*   *Protein: 91.6 g*

Week 2 – Day 1

Breakfast – Berry Shake

Lunch – Southwest Salsa Eggs, Baked Spinach Chips

Dinner – Spinach Almond Salad, Fresh Strawberry Limeade

Snack – Low-Carb Cacao Macarons

Snack – Balsamic & Avocado Snack

1960 calories

Net Carbs: 59.3 g

Total Fat: 147 g

Protein: 83.8 g

Macros: 18% C | 68% F | 14% P

Week 2 – Day 2

Breakfast – English Paleo Muffins

Lunch – Low-Carb Skillet Pizza

Dinner – Squash & Zucchini Casserole

Snack – Winter Strawberry Ricotta

Snack – Keto Avocado Brownies

1717 calories

Macros: 17% C | 65% F | 18% P

Net Carbs: 54.8 g   Total Fat: 124.8 g   Protein: 95.1 g

Week 2 – Day 3

Breakfast – Keto Breakfast Tacos [remove bacon and recalculate nutrition info]

Lunch – Cauliflower "Mac" & Cheese

Dinner – Keto Eggroll in a Bowl, Keto Egg Drop Soup

Snack – Keto Protein Shake

Snack – Dark Chocolate Raspberry Fat Bombs

1946 calories

Net Carbs: 41.2 g

Total Fat: 147.6 g

Protein: 104 g

Macros: 12% C | 68% F | 20% P

Week 2 – Day 4

Breakfast – Berry Shake

Lunch – Low-Carb Pancakes, Egg Mushroom Cups, Orange

Dinner – Easy Dinner Parmesan Zucchini, Low-Carb Onion Rings

Snack – Low-Carb Crackers

Snack – Peanut Butter Chocolate Fat Bombs

1931 calories

Net Carbs: 50.2 g

Total Fat: 147.2 g

Protein: 96.3 g

Macros: 14% C | 69% F | 17% P

Week 2 – Day 5

Breakfast – Bulletproof Coffee

Lunch – Pesto Scrambled Eggs, Zucchetti

Dinner – Creamy Garlic Mushrooms, Tomato & Basil Salad

Snack – Protein-Boosted Yogurt

Snack – Chocolate Fat Bombs

1848 calories

Net Carbs: 38.8 g

Total Fat: 145.2 g

Protein: 93.8 g

Macros: 10% C | 71% F | 19% P

Week 2 – Day 6

Breakfast – Low-Carb Maple Pecan Pancakes

Lunch – Cauliflower-Crusted Grilled Cheese Sandwich

Dinner – Baked Parmesan Tomatoes, Superfood Keto Soup

Snack – Raspberry Greek Yogurt

Snack – Mint Fudge Fat Bombs

1866 calories

Net Carbs: 48.5 g

Total Fat: 149.2 g

Protein: 81.3 g

Macros: 13% C | 72% F | 15% P

Week 2 – Day 7

Breakfast – Sweet Egg Pancakes

Lunch – Baby Kale & Blackberry Salad

Dinner - Feta-Stuffed Portobello Mushroom, Cloud Bread

Snack – Peanut Butter Chocolate Fat Bombs

Snack – Low-Carb Blueberry Muffin

1803 calories

Net Carbs: 48.6 g

Total Fat: 135.4 g

Protein: 91.4 g

Macros: 15% C | 68% F | 17% P

Recipes

Keto Lemon Blueberry Muffins

Yields: 12 servings (Serving Size: 1 muffin)

Ingredients

1 tsp Lemon zest

¼ cup Butter

2 cups Almond flour

1 cup, Heavy whipping cream

2 large Eggs

1 tbsp Stevia Sweetener

1 tsp Baking powder

½ cup Blueberries

Directions

Preheat oven to 350 F. Zest lemon, and melt butter. Crack eggs into a large mixing bowl, and whisk until well-mixed. Add all other ingredients into the mixing bowl with eggs, and mix until well combined. Pour muffins into 12 paper or silicone baking cups. Bake for 25-30 minutes, until golden brown and a toothpick inserted in the middle of a muffin comes out clean. Serve cold or warm.

Spinach and Cheese Omelet

Yields: 1 omelet

Ingredients

1 spray Pam cooking spray

2 medium Eggs

1 cup Spinach

Dash of Salt

Dash of Pepper

2 oz Cheddar cheese

Directions

Whisk the eggs, then add the spinach, salt, and pepper. Coat a skillet with cooking spray. Heat pan over medium heat, then add the egg mixture. Cook until eggs are almost completely set. Carefully flip the omelet, then add the cheese on top. Cover the pan briefly to melt cheese. Serve warm.

Keto Mushroom Chips

Yields: 1 serving

Ingredients

1.5 large Mushrooms

3 tsp Clarified butter (ghee)

Dash of Salt

Dash of Pepper

Directions

Preheat the oven to 300 F. Slice the mushrooms thinly with a knife (or mandolin). On a non-stick baking sheet (or other pan coated with non-stick spray), place the mushrooms in a single layer. As the mushrooms will shrink while cooking, you do not need to leave space between each. Brush each mushroom with melted ghee, then sprinkle with salt and pepper. Bake for 45 to 60 minutes, rotating the tray 2 to 3 times for even baking, or until mushrooms are crispy and golden brown. Cool to room temperature and serve.

5-Minute Keto Pizza

Yields: 1 serving

Ingredients

2 tbsp Parmesan cheese

1 1/2 tbsp Psyllium husk

2 tbsp Basil (fresh)

2 extra large Eggs

2 tsp Olive oil

1 1/2 oz Mozzarella cheese

3 tbsp Tomato sauce

Add dry ingredients to a large mixing bowl that will fit your immersion blender. Add eggs and mix well using immersion blender. Continue blending for about 30 seconds, allowing psyllium husk to absorb some of the liquid. Over medium-high, heat olive oil in a pan. Once hot, spoon egg mixture into the pan and spread into a circular shape to create your "crust". When edges have set and the mixture begins to brown, flip (or transfer to a plate and flip), then heat the other side for 30-60 seconds. Turn broiler to high. Spread tomato sauce over crust, then add cheese. Put the pizza in the oven to broil, and leave the door open slightly so you can keep an eye on it. Remove from oven once cheese starts to bubble. Top with freshly chopped basil and serve hot.

Spinach Salad with Blackberries

Yields: 1 serving

Ingredients

2 cups Spinach

2 large Scallions

2 tbsp Olive oil

Dash of Pepper

Juice of 1 Lemon

½ cup Blackberries

Directions

Wash spinach well, drain, chop, and squeeze out excess water. Chop green onions. Add spinach, scallions, oil, pepper, and lemon juice in a bowl. Toss and top with blackberries.

Keto Protein Shake

Yields: 1 serving

Ingredients

1 cup Water

1 scoop (30g) Protein powder

Directions

Add protein powder to water – using a shaker cup, blender, or stirring with a spoon. If your protein powder is unflavored, add a little bit of sweetener and cocoa powder to improve the taste.

Dark Chocolate Raspberry Fat Bombs

Yields: 15 servings

Serving Size: 1 fat bomb

Ingredients

4 oz Cocoa butter

¼ cup Coconut oil

4¼ oz Dark chocolate

⅓ cup Cocoa

1 tsp Aspartame

30 Raspberries

30 Almonds

¾ tbsp Vanilla extract

Directions

Place the almonds in a pan and toast for about 5 minutes. Place one almond into each raspberry, spread over a tray, and place in the freezer for about an hour. Place the cocoa butter, coconut oil, and unsweetened chocolate in a bowl over a pot of water and bring to boil. Use a double boiler if you have one – otherwise, make sure the water doesn't touch the bowl. Allow chocolate mixture to melt, and stir. Once the chocolate mixture is melted, add the unsweetened cocoa powder, sweetener, and vanilla. Mix until well combined, and set aside. Place small muffin cups on a baking tray and pour 1 tablespoon of the chocolate mixture into each of them. Add 2 frozen raspberries filled with almonds into each cup. Pour another tablespoon of the chocolate over them, covering the raspberries completely. The chocolate will start to solidify instantly. Place in the fridge for about 30 minutes or until set. Store the fat bombs in the fridge to keep them fresh in the fridge for up to 3 days or store in the freezer for longer.

Bulletproof Coffee

Yields: 1 serving

Ingredients

10 fl oz Coffee

1 tbsp Butter

1 tbsp Coconut oil or MCT oil

Directions

Grind and brew coffee in French press or coffee machine. While coffee is brewing, place butter and coconut oil into coffee cup. Pour coffee into cup, and wait 1 minute for butter and oil to dissolve partially. Stir to combine, and wait about 1 minute until fully dissolved. Serve immediately, stirring when necessary as oil and fat separate. Serve hot.

Coconut Flour Waffles

Yields: 1 serving

Serving Size: 2 waffles

Ingredients

2 extra large Eggs

⅛ cup Butter

1 tbsp Coconut flour

¾ tsp Salt

Dash of Baking soda

1 tbsp Coconut milk

⅛ tbsp Honey

Directions

Heat waffle maker. In a large bowl, beat eggs with an electric mixer for about 30 seconds, until eggs are well-beaten. Add melted butter slowly while mixing. Add coconut flour, salt, baking soda, and coconut milk. Mix for 45 seconds on low, until the batter begins to thicken. Cook waffles according to your waffle maker's specifications. Serve with honey.

Herbed Lemon Tofu

Yields: 1 serving

Ingredients

½ lb Tofu

1 tbsp Lemon juice

1/4 tbsp Vinegar

1 tbsp Soy sauce

1 tbsp Olive oil

1 tsp Thyme (ground)

Dash of Pepper

Directions

Preheat the oven to 475 F. Wrap the block of tofu in paper towels and press for 10 minutes by adding weight on top (a heavy pan or some canned food work nicely). Remove the paper towels, and cut the tofu into ½"-thick pieces. Combine the remaining ingredients in a small bowl, and whisk together well. Add tofu to a casserole or baking dish in a single layer, then cover with the liquid mixture, turning once to coat.

Bake tofu for 30 to 40 minutes, or until browned, turning once halfway through baking.

Roasted Cauliflower and Tahini

Yields: 1 serving

Ingredients

1/4 cup chopped Cauliflower (½" pieces)

1/4 tbsp Sesame butter

Directions

Preheat oven to 425 F. Toss cauliflower pieces with sesame butter. Spread in pan, and roast for about 20 minutes or until lightly toasty brown.

Mediterranean Omelet with Fennel, Olives, & Dill

Yields: 2 omelets

Serving Size: 1 omelet

Ingredients

2 tbsp Olive oil

¼ cup Olives

2 oz Goat cheese

8 Cherry tomatoes

1½ tbsp Dill

2 cups Fennel (sliced)

5 extra large Eggs

Dash of Pepper

Dash of Salt

Directions

Remove fennel fronds, chop, and reserve. Thinly slice fennel. Coarsely crumble goat cheese. Coarsely chop olives and dill. Beat eggs well, and season to taste with salt and pepper. Heat 1 tbsp oil in 10-inch nonstick skillet over medium-high heat. Add fennel bulb, and sauté until beginning to brown, about 5 minutes. Cover and cook until softened, stirring occasionally, about 4 minutes. Add tomatoes and mash with fork, then mix in olives. Season with salt and pepper. Transfer mixture to medium bowl. Add remaining 1 tbsp oil to same skillet; heat over medium-high heat. Add beaten eggs and cook until eggs are just set in center, tilting skillet and lifting edges of omelet with spatula to let uncooked portion flow underneath, about 3 minutes. Sprinkle half of cheese over half of omelet, then top with fennel mixture. Sprinkle dill on top, then remaining cheese. Using spatula, fold the uncovered half of omelet over cheese; slide onto plate. Garnish with chopped fennel fronds and serve.

Grilled Asparagus

Yields: 1 serving

Ingredients

4 oz Asparagus

¼ tbsp Olive oil

Dash of Salt

Dash of Pepper

Directions

Heat grill to medium. Coat asparagus with olive oil and season with salt and pepper Grill for 2 to 3 minutes or until tender.

Cheese Cubes

Yields: 1 serving

Ingredients

1 oz Cheddar cheese

Directions

Cut cheese into cubes.

Strawberry Cheesecake Fat Bombs

Yields: 4 servings   *Serving Size: 3 fat bombs*

Ingredients

¾ cup Cream cheese

¼ cup Butter

½ cup Strawberries (whole)

¼ tsp Stevia Sweetener

1 tbsp Vanilla extract

Directions

Cut butter into small pieces. Add butter pieces and cream cheese to mixing bowl. Leave at room temperature for 30–60 minutes until softened. Meanwhile, wash the strawberries and remove the green parts. Place them into a bowl and mash using a fork or place in a blender for a smooth texture. Add the stevia and vanilla extract, and mix well. Before you mix the strawberries with the remaining ingredients, make sure they have reached room temperature. Add strawberries to the bowl with softened butter and cream cheese. Use a hand whisk or food processor and mix until well combined. Spoon the mixture into small muffin silicon molds or candy molds. Place in the freezer for about 2 hours or until set. When done, unmold the fat bombs and place into a container. Keep in the freezer and serve cold.

Cream Cheese Pancakes

Yields: 1 serving

Ingredients

2 oz Cream cheese

2 large Eggs

1 tsp Cinnamon

⅓ oz Coconut flour

1 packet Stevia

Directions

Add all ingredients to a blender and mix well. Cook like a regular pancake on a buttered or greased non-stick skillet over medium high heat until both sides are golden brown.

Avocado Egg Bake

Yields: 1 serving

Ingredients

1 medium Avocado

1 large Egg

Dash of Salt

Dash of Pepper

Directions

Preheat oven to 425 F. Halve the avocado, and scoop some fruit out to widen the hole. Crack an egg into a bowl and scoop the yolk into one avocado half. Divide, and scoop in any egg white you can fit into the two halves. Bake for 15-20 minutes until egg is set. Season with salt and pepper and serve.

Cloud Bread

Yields: 6 servings

Serving Size: 1/6 loaf

Ingredients

6 large Eggs

½ tsp Cream of tartar

¾ cup Sour cream

½ tsp Baking soda

¼ tsp Garlic powder

¼ tsp Onion powder

¼ tsp Salt

2 scoops (60 g) unflavored Protein powder

<u>Directions</u>

Preheat oven to 300 F. Crack and separate egg yolks from whites. Place egg whites in a stand mixer with cream of tartar, and whip until stiff peaks. Set aside. Place egg yolks in a bowl with remaining ingredients, and stir well to combine. Fold a small amount of egg whites into the yolk mixture a little at a time until it's all incorporated. Pour this mixture into a greased loaf pan. Bake for 60 minutes, or until a toothpick or skewer stick in the center comes out clean. Allow to cool before removing from pan and slicing. Best if toasted. Keep refrigerated.

Tomato & Basil Salad

Yields: 2 servings

Serving Size: 1 salad

<u>Ingredients</u>

5 Plum tomatoes

5 tbsp Basil (fresh, chopped)

1 cup Onions (chopped)

1 cup Mozzarella cheese (cubed)

4 tsp Balsamic vinegar

4 tbsp Olive oil

Dash of Pepper

Dash of Salt

Directions

Wash and dice tomatoes. Chop basil. Peel and dice onion. Combine vinegar, oil, and basil, and toss to combine in a large bowl. Add tomatoes, onion, cheese, and toss to coat. Serve right away, or put in refrigerator for 1 hour to marry the flavors.

Baked Spinach Chips

Yields: 1 serving

Ingredients

4 cups Spinach

Dash of Salt

1 tbsp Olive oil

Directions

Preheat oven to 350 F. Mix all ingredients together in a bowl, until spinach is evenly coated. Bake for 15 minutes, or until edges of spinach start to brown. Allow to cool.

Strawberries

Yields: 1 serving

Ingredients

1 cup Strawberries (whole)

Directions

Wash and eat. Easy peasy.

Mint Fudge Fat Bombs

Yields: 16 servings

Serving Size: 1 fat bomb

Ingredients

1½ cups Coconut oil

1½ cups Pumpkin and squash seeds

½ cup Parsley (dried)

2 tsp Vanilla extract

1 tsp Peppermint (fresh)

¼ tsp Salt

Directions

Melt coconut oil in small saucepan. Add remaining ingredients to blender, add coconut oil, and blend until smooth. Pour into an 8×8 baking pan and freeze until solid. Cut into squares once set. Store in refrigerator to prevent softening.

Keto Pumpkin Protein Bars

Yields: 4 servings

Serving Size: 1 bar

Ingredients

4 scoops (120 g) Protein powder

½ cup Pumpkin

½ cup Cream cheese

1 extra large Egg

½ tbsp Pumpkin pie spice

Directions

Preheat oven to 350 F. Grease a loaf pan (or use a cooking spray to coat sides). Mash pumpkin and cream cheese together. Stir in protein powder until thoroughly combined. Add egg and mix until the dough becomes similar to pancake batter. Pour into your loaf pan and bake for 20 minutes. Let cool and slice.

Low-Carb Asiago Baked Eggs

Yields: 2 servings

Serving Size: 1 ramekin/bowl

Ingredients

4 tbsp Butter

4 large Eggs

1 oz Asiago Italian cheese (grated)

Directions

Preheat oven to 350 F. Using a small amount of the butter, butter two ramekins (or 2-cup baking bowls). Split the remaining butter between prepared bowls. Place one ramekin in the microwave for about 30 seconds on high to melt butter. Repeat with other. Drop two whole eggs into each bowl. Top each with 1 tablespoon of grated Asiago cheese. Bake in oven for 15 minutes or until egg whites become white. Serve hot.

Kale Chips

Yields: 1 serving

Ingredients

2 cups Kale   ½ tbsp Olive oil   ⅛ tsp Salt

Directions

Preheat oven to 350 F. Remove center ribs and stems from kale if present. Tear kale leaves into 3-4" inch pieces. Toss kale leaves in olive oil and salt. Spread on baking sheet coated with cooking spray. Bake for 12-15 minutes until browned around edges and crispy.

Caramelized Cauliflower Steaks

Yields: 4 servings

Serving Size: 1 steak

Ingredients

1 large head Cauliflower

½ cup Olive oil

1 tsp Salt

1 tsp Pepper

1 Lemon, seeds removed

Directions

Preheat oven to 350 F. Use a sharp, heavy knife to cut cauliflower into 1"-thick steaks, starting at the center of the cauliflower head and cutting through the stem end, from top to base. You should have four steak slices total. (Cook the extra pieces along with your steaks, as they are still great to eat.) Lay the four steaks on a baking sheet, brush them with olive oil, and sprinkle with salt and pepper. Heat the remainder of the oil in a large skillet over medium-high heat. Place as many of the steaks in the skillet as will comfortably fit. Fry for 2-3 minutes on each side or until golden brown and slightly softened; then, return the steak to the baking sheet. Repeat until all the steaks are cooked. Place the baking sheet in the oven and bake until the cauliflower steaks are tender, 10-15 minutes. Serve with lemon wedges, either hot or at room temperature.

Quick and Easy Low-Carb Caprese Salad

Yields: 1 serving

Ingredients

4 Cherry tomatoes

½ cup Mozzarella cheese (cubed)

1 tbsp Olive oil

1 tbsp Basil (fresh, chopped)

Directions

Slice tomatoes and mozzarella. Drizzle with olive oil. Thinly slice basil and sprinkle on top. Serve immediately.

Chocolate Fat Bombs

Yields: 4 servings

Serving Size: 5 fat bombs

Ingredients

1 cup Coconut oil

½ cup Cocoa powder

1 tbsp Honey

1 tsp Salt

Directions

Process all ingredients together in a food processor until mixture is smooth and creamy. Pour into small-sized ice cube trays or silicone molds, and freeze. Once frozen, pop the fat bombs out of the molds and store them in a freezer zip-top bag or jar.

Greek Yogurt with Blueberries, Walnuts, & Honey

Yields: 1 serving

Ingredients

¼ cup Blueberries

1 tsp Honey

¼ cup Walnuts (chopped)

½ cup Greek yogurt

Directions

Mix ingredients together and serve.

Iced Coffee Protein Shake

Yields: 1 serving

Ingredients

2 cups Coffee

1 scoop (30 g) Protein powder

1 cup Ice cubes

Directions

Brew coffee and cool. Combine all ingredients in a blender, and pulse until smooth.

Cucumber Avocado Salad

Yields: 1 serving

Ingredients

1 cup Lettuce (shredded)

8 Cherry tomatoes

¼ cup Cucumber (sliced)

1 Avocado (seeded, peeled)

3 rings (3" x ¼") Red bell pepper

1½ tbsp Lemon juice

Directions

Chop all ingredients and toss well. Serve cold.

Low-Carb Jalapeno Cheese Crisps

Yields: 4 servings

Ingredients

5 Jalapeno peppers

2 tbsp Olive oil

½ tsp Onion powder (or salt)

6 slices (6 oz) Swiss cheese

Dash of Pepper

Directions

Preheat oven to 450 F. Slice jalapeno into thin slices (about ½" thick). Remove seeds if you don't like food too spicy. Toss jalapeno slices with olive oil and onion powder (or salt) and arrange flat on baking tray with parchment paper. Bake for 10 to 15 minutes or until jalapeno slices are crispy. This is why it's important to cut them thin. Remove from oven and allow to cool, blotting with a towel to remove excess oil. Increase oven temperature to 400 F. Re-line baking sheet with parchment paper. Tear cheese slices into several pieces, then fold each piece around a jalapeno slice. Make sure the slices are still flat – not round. Place slices on baking sheet. Bake at 400 F for about 6-7 minutes, or until cheese is crispy (start checking around 5 minutes). Remove from oven, cool, then season with pepper.

Asparagus, Fontina, & Tomato Frittata

Yields: 2 servings

Serving Size: ½ frittata

Ingredients

6 extra large Eggs

2 tbsp Heavy whipping cream

½ tsp Salt

¼ tsp Pepper

1 tbsp Olive oil

1½ cups Asparagus

1 tbsp Butter

1 medium Tomato (whole)

½ cup Fontina cheese (diced)

Directions

Preheat the broiler. Whisk the eggs, cream, salt, and pepper in a medium bowl to blend. Set aside. Chop the asparagus and tomato. Heat the oil and butter in a nonstick oven-proof skillet over medium heat. Add the asparagus, and sauté until crisp-tender, about 2 minutes. Raise the heat to medium-high. Add the tomato and a pinch of salt, and sauté 2 minutes longer. Pour the egg mixture over the asparagus mixture, and cook for a few minutes until the eggs start to set. Sprinkle with cheese. Reduce heat to medium-low and cook until the frittata is almost set but the top is still runny, about 2 minutes. Place the skillet under the broiler. Broil until the top is set and golden brown on top, about 5 minutes. Let the frittata stand 2 minutes. Loosen the frittata from the skillet and slide the frittata onto a plate. Serve warm.

Pecans

Yields: 1 serving

Ingredients

1 oz (about 19 halves) Pecans

Directions

Just Enjoy!

Grilled Peaches with Honey

Yields: 6 servings

Serving Size: ½ Peach

Ingredients

3 medium (2⅔" diameter) Peaches

1 tbsp Olive oil

1 tbsp Honey

Directions

Preheat grill to high. Cut peaches in half; remove pits. Brush cut side of peach halves with olive oil, and place on grill, cut side down. Grill until golden brown and caramelized, about 2 to 3 minutes. Turn peach halves over, and grill until slightly soft and just warmed through, about 2 minutes longer. Remove from grill and drizzle with honey.

Avocado Egg Stack

Yields: 1 serving

Ingredients

1 tsp Salt

1 Avocado

1 tbsp Olive oil

1 extra large Egg

Directions

Slice avocado, and put on plate. Salt if desired. Fry egg in olive oil to desired preference; serve on avocado slices.

Low-Carb Spicy Nachos

Yields: 4 servings

Ingredients

6 slices (1 oz each) Cheddar cheese

½ Avocado

½ cup Tomatoes (chopped or sliced)

3 tbsp Onions (chopped)

1 tsp Paprika

½ tsp Garlic salt

½ tsp Cumin (ground)

1 tbsp Cayenne pepper

Directions

To make the cheese "chips", preheat the oven to 400 F. Cut the cheddar cheese slices into quarters and place on baking sheets lined with parchment paper, about 2" apart. Bake for 5 to 8 minutes, until crispy and slightly browned. Pat lightly with a paper towel to soak up excess oil. Set aside to cool. Meanwhile, dice the avocado, tomatoes, and onions. Mix the spices together, then stir into the mixture. After the chips have cooled for at least 15 minutes and are crispy, top them with spoonfuls of the topping mixture. Sprinkle a couple shreds of mozzarella cheese on top of each chip.

Zucchini Alfredo

Yields: 4 servings

Ingredients

1 large Zucchini

1 tbsp Olive oil

3 tbsp Cream cheese

1 tbsp Sour cream

¼ cup Parmesan cheese (grated)

Directions

Use a spiralizer or vegetable peeler to make zucchini noodles. Heat olive oil in a large pan over medium heat. Add zucchini noodles to pan and sauté for about 5 minutes. Remove noodles to serving dish. Add cream cheese, sour cream, and Parmesan cheese to the pan and stir to combine. Let cook until homogenous and heated evenly through. Pour sauce over noodles and toss to combine. Top with additional Parmesan cheese, if desired.

Chia Cottage Cheese with Blueberries

Yields: 1 serving

Ingredients

1 cup Cottage cheese (small curd)

½ cup Blueberries

2 tbsp Chia seeds

Directions

Put the cottage cheese in a bowl, add the blueberries, and stir well. Sprinkle with chia seeds. Stir together once more, and serve.

Spinach Avocado Smoothie Bowl

Yields: 1 serving

Ingredients

4 cups Spinach

1 Avocado

1 ⅓ cups Coconut milk (unsweetened)

Directions

Blend and serve with any desired toppings.

Cauliflower-Crusted Grilled Cheese Sandwich

Yields: 2 servings

Serving Size: 1 sandwich

Ingredients

1 small head Cauliflower

1 large Egg

½ cup Parmesan cheese (grated)

1 tsp Oregano (dried)

4 slices (1 oz each) Cheddar cheese

Directions

Preheat oven to 450 F. Place cauliflower into food processor, and pulse until crumbs about half the size of a grain of rice. Alternatively, you can do this by hand with a box grater. Place cauliflower into large microwave-safe bowl, and microwave for 2 minutes until soft and tender. Stir cauliflower, and place back into the microwave, cooking for another 3 minutes. Remove and stir again, and return to the microwave, cooking for another 5 minutes. At this point, you should see the cauliflower is starting to become drier. Microwave for another 5 minutes. Cauliflower should still be slightly moist to the touch, but should look dry and clumped. Add gg, parmesan and seasoning. Stir to combine until a smooth paste forms. Divide dough into 4 equal parts. Place onto large baking sheet lined with parchment paper. Using your knuckles and fingers, shape into square bread slices about ½" thick. Bake cauliflower bread for about 15-18 minutes or until golden brown. Remove from oven and let cool a few minutes. Using a good spatula, carefully slide cauliflower bread off of parchment paper. Make 2 cauliflower sandwiches by adding 2 slices of cheese in between each pair of bread slices. Place sandwiches into toaster oven and broil for 5-10 minutes, or until cheese is completely melted and bread is toasty. If you don't own a toaster oven, you can also do this in the oven under the broiler.

Parmesan & Mushroom Baked Eggs

Yields: 2 servings

Serving Size: 2 eggs

Ingredients

1 tbsp Olive oil

2 cups Mushrooms (sliced)

Dash of Salt

Dash of Pepper

4 extra large Eggs

2 tsp Parmesan cheese (grated)

Directions

Preheat oven to 400 F. Spray 2 individual baking dishes or a flat casserole dish with non-stick spray. Wash mushrooms and pat dry. Slice mushrooms into slices about ½" thick. Heat oil in a large frying pan over high heat and sauté mushrooms until they have released all their liquid and the liquid has evaporated, about 6-8 minutes. Season mushrooms with a little salt and fresh ground black pepper and quickly transfer to baking dishes. Break two eggs over the mushrooms in each individual dish (or four eggs over all the mushrooms in a casserole dish). Season eggs with a little salt and fresh ground black pepper to taste, and sprinkle with Parmesan cheese. Bake eggs until they are done to your liking, about 10 minutes for firm whites and partly-soft yolks. Serve hot.

Easy Sautéed Eggplant

Yields: 2 servings

Serving Size: ½ cup

Ingredients

1 cup Eggplant (diced)

4 tbsp Olive oil

2 cloves Garlic (minced)

Dash of Salt

Directions

Peel and dice eggplant (about ½" cubes). Coat large skillet with olive oil over medium-high heat. Sauté eggplant cubes for 4-5 minutes, until tender. Add minced garlic, and toss for a few minutes. Remove from heat. Salt to taste. Can be served hot or cold.

Protein-Boosted Yogurt

Yields: 1 serving

Ingredients

1 scoop (30 g) Protein powder

8 oz Greek yogurt

Directions

Mix a scoop of your favorite protein powder into yogurt for a quick protein snack.

Berry Shake

Yields: 1 serving

Ingredients

½ cup Coconut milk (unsweetened)

½ scoop (15 g) Protein powder

⅓ cup frozen Blackberries (unthawed)

2 tbsp Flaxseed (whole)

¾ cup Water

1 tsp Honey

Directions

Blend all ingredients in a blender. Serve cold.

Southwest Salsa Eggs

Yields: 1 serving

Ingredients

2 sprays Pam spray

4 large Eggs

2 tbsp Salsa

Directions

Spray pan and heat to medium. Crack eggs into pan, and scramble. Lower heat to medium-low. Add salsa, and stir until firm. Serve warm.

Fresh Strawberry Limeade

Yields: 8 servings

Serving Size: 1 cup

Ingredients

1 cup Strawberries (whole)

3 Limes

2½ oz Agave nectar

2 cups Water

1 liter (34 fl oz) Club soda

Directions

Add fresh strawberries, limes, agave, and water to a blender. Blend until smooth. Using a strainer to catch chunks, pour strawberry-lime mixture into a pitcher. Add club soda to strawberry limeade, and add ice. Serve cold.

Spinach Almond Salad

Yields: 1 serving

Ingredients

3 extra large Eggs

1½ cups Spinach

½ cup Broccoli (chopped)

1 cup Cherry tomatoes

2 tbsp Almonds (sliced)

Directions

Place eggs in a pot. Cover with water, bring to a boil, remove from heat, cover, and let sit 10 minutes. Drain, peel, chop, and set aside. Add spinach to a large salad bowl. Chop broccoli, tomatoes, and hard-boiled eggs and add to salad bowl. Sprinkle with slivered almonds. Top with your favorite dressing and serve.

Balsamic & Avocado Snack

Yields: 2 servings

Serving Size: ½ avocado

Ingredients

2 tbsp Olive oil

1 tbsp Balsamic vinegar

1 Avocado

Directions

Stir together oil and vinegar. Cut the avocado in half, and discard the pit; divide the sauce between the avocado halves. Eat with a spoon.

Low-Carb Cacao Macarons

Yields: 2 servings

Serving Size: 3 macarons

Ingredients

3 oz Coconut meat

1 oz Dark chocolate cacao nibs

1 Egg white

1 tbsp Agave nectar

1 tbsp Vanilla extract

Directions

Preheat oven to 400 F. Put coconut in a small bowl. Add cacao nibs. Add egg white, 2-3 tsp of sweetener, and vanilla extract. Mix. Press mixture into a tablespoon, invert on baking sheet and tap. Bake for about 11 minutes or until golden brown.

English Paleo Muffins

Yields: 1 serving (2 muffins)

Ingredients

½ cup Sunflower seed flour

½ tsp Baking soda

¼ tsp Salt

2 extra large Eggs

1 tbsp Coconut oil

2 tbsp Almond butter

4 tbsp Water

Directions

Whisk together the dry ingredients in a small bowl. Add the remaining wet ingredients, and whisk again until fully incorporated. Transfer the mixture into 2 greased microwave-safe ramekins. Microwave for 2 minutes. Remove muffins from the ramekins, slice the muffins in half, and toast for 2-3 minutes in a toaster oven. Serve with almond butter.

Low-Carb Skillet Pizza

Yields: 1 serving

Ingredients

¾ cup Mozzarella cheese (shredded)

2 tbsp Tomatoes (crushed)

¼ tsp Garlic powder

¼ tsp Italian seasoning

1 tbsp Parmesan cheese (shredded)

Directions

Heat small nonstick skillet over medium. Cover the bottom of hot skillet evenly with shredded mozzarella cheese. This will be your crust. Lightly spread the crushed tomatoes on top of the cheese, using the back of a spoon, and leaving a border around the edges of the cheese crust. Sprinkle with garlic powder and Italian seasoning. Cook until sizzling, bubbled, and edges are brown. Try to lift up the edges of the pizza with a spatula. When it is ready, it will easily lift up from the pan. If it sticks, that means it's not quite ready. Keep lifting and checking frequently. When it finally starts to lift up easily without sticking, work spatula gently and slowly underneath to loosen up entire pizza and transfer to a cutting board. Sprinkle lightly with Parmesan. Allow to cool for about 5 minutes. The crust will firm up even more while it cools. Cut with a pizza cutter, transfer to a serving plate, and serve.

Squash & Zucchini Casserole

Yields: 4 servings

Ingredients

Dash of Pepper

Dash of Salt

2 cups Romano cheese (grated)

2 medium Yellow squash

2 medium Onions

2 large Zucchini

½ cup Butter

4 large Tomatoes

Directions

Thinly slice onion. Slice tomatoes evenly. Preheat oven to 375 F. Cut the zucchini and squash into long, thin layers. Lightly grease a 7x11-inch baking dish and layer the squash, zucchini, onion and tomatoes into the baking dish. Sprinkle with cheese and add pats of butter between each layer of vegetables, and season each layer with salt and ground black pepper to taste. Continue this layering process until all the vegetables are used up and top this off with the remaining butter and cheese. Cover and bake at 375 F for 20 to 30 minutes, or until vegetables are to desired tenderness and cheese is melted and bubbly. Serve warm.

Winter Strawberry Ricotta

Yields: 1 serving

Ingredients

6 Strawberries

1 packet Sucralose (or other sugar-free sweetener)

⅓ cup Ricotta cheese

Directions

Thaw strawberries in the microwave so they are slightly warmed, about 75 seconds on defrost. Add the sweetener and ricotta cheese, and serve.

Keto Avocado Brownies

Yields: 9 servings

Serving Size: 1 brownie

Ingredients

2 Avocado

½ tsp Vanilla extract

¼ cup Cocoa powder

1 tsp Stevia sweetener

3 tbsp Coconut oil

2 extra large Eggs

⅔ cup or approx. (6 oz) Semi-sweet chocolate chips

¾ cup Almond flour

¼ tsp Baking soda

1 tsp Baking powder

¼ cup Walnuts (chopped)

¼ tsp Salt

1½ oz Truvia Baking Blend

Directions

Preheat oven to 350 F and prepare a baking pan with parchment; set aside. Peel the avocado and place in a food processor. Process until smooth. Add each ingredient one at a time and process for a few seconds until all of the ingredients (excluding dry) have been added to the processor. Combine dry ingredients in a separate bowl, whisk together. Add to the food processor and mix until combined. Pour into prepared pan and bake for about 35 minutes.

Keto Breakfast Tacos

Yield: 3 servings

Serving Size: 1 taco

Ingredients

1 cup Mozzarella cheese (diced)

6 large Eggs

2 tbsp Butter

1 tsp Salt

1 tsp Salt

½ Avocado

1 oz Cheddar cheese (shredded)

Directions

Heat ⅓ cup mozzarella at a time on a clean pan at medium heat. This cheese will form our taco shells. Wait until the cheese is browned on the edges (about 2-3 minutes), then slide a spatula under it to unstick it. (This should happen easily if you're using whole-milk mozzarella, as the oil from the cheese will prevent it from sticking.) Use a pair of tongs to lift the shell up and drape it over a wooden spoon resting on a pot. Do the same with the rest of your cheese, working in batches of ⅓ cup. Next, cook your eggs in the butter, stirring occasionally until they're done. Season with salt and pepper. Spoon a third of your scrambled eggs into each hardened taco shell. Then add sliced avocado on top. Sprinkle cheddar cheese over the tops of the breakfast tacos.

Cauliflower "Mac" & Cheese

Yields: 6 servings

Ingredients

1 large head Cauliflower

2 tbsp Coconut oil

2 tsp Salt

2 tsp Pepper

1 cup Heavy whipping cream

2 oz Cream cheese

2 cups Cheddar cheese (shredded)

¼ tsp Garlic powder

½ tbsp Mustard seed

¼ tsp Pepper

Directions

Preheat oven to 400 F. Drizzle melted coconut oil over cauliflower. Season with salt and pepper and toss to combine well. Bake for about 20 minutes. Remove from oven and move to a casserole dish. Reduce oven temperature to 375 F. Heat cream to a simmer. Add cream cheese (in chunks) and 1½ cups cheddar cheese (reserve ½ cup for later), add garlic powder mustard seed, and white pepper; whisk/stir well until all melted. Pour mix into baking dish with cauliflower, mix well. Cover with remaining ½ cup cheddar. Bake uncovered for 15-20 minutes.

Keto Eggroll in a Bowl

Yields: 4 servings

Ingredients

1 medium head Cabbage

1 medium Onion

1 tbsp Sesame oil

¼ cup Soy sauce

1 clove Garlic (minced)

1 tsp Ginger root

2 tbsp Vegetable broth

Dash of Salt

Dash of Pepper

2 stalks Scallions

Directions

Ensure cabbage and onion are thinly sliced into long strands. Use a spiralizer to cut the vegetables for quickest results. Add sesame oil and onion to pan. Mix together and continue cooking over medium heat. Mix soy sauce, garlic, and ground ginger together in a small bowl. Once onions have browned, add the sauce mixture to the pan. Immediately add the cabbage mixture to the pan and toss to coat the vegetable and evenly distribute ingredients. Add broth to the pan and mix. Continue cooking over medium heat for three minutes, stirring frequently. Garnish with salt, pepper, and chopped green onion.

Keto Egg Drop Soup

Yields: 1 serving

Ingredients

2 tbsp Butter

4 large Eggs

1 tsp Garlic powder

1 tsp Chili powder

3 cups Vegetable broth

Directions

Heat a skillet on medium-high. Add in the broth and butter. Bring the broth to a boil and stir everything together. Then, add the chili and garlic powder and stir again. Turn off the stove. Beat the eggs in a separate container and pour into the steaming broth. Stir together well and let sit for a moment to finish cooking. Serve hot.

Berry Shake

Yields: 1 serving

Ingredients

½ cup Coconut milk (unsweetened)

½ scoop (15 g) Protein powder

⅓ cup frozen Blackberries (unthawed)

2 tbsp Flaxseed (whole)

¾ cup Water

1 tsp Honey

Directions

Blend all ingredients in a blender. Serve cold.

Low-Carb Pancakes

Yields: 1 serving

Ingredients

1 scoop (30 g) Protein powder

Dash of Salt

2 extra large Eggs

2 tsp Olive oil

4 tbsp Water

2 sprays Pam cooking spray

Directions

Whisk all of the ingredients (except water and cooking spray), in a small bowl until smooth. Meanwhile, lightly grease a small nonstick skillet with oil or cooking spray and heat on medium. Add up to 1 tbsp of water if you'd like a thinner batter. Pour in the batter and tilt the pan to spread the batter evenly over the bottom of the skillet. When bubbles appear all over the pancake and the batter on top looks like it's starting to set up carefully work a spatula around the edges and then under the pancake to flip it over. Cook until the second side is lightly browned. Don't let it get too dark or it may taste bitter.

Egg Mushroom Cups

Yields: 2 servings

Serving Size: 1 mushroom

Ingredients

2 Portobella mushrooms (whole)

1 tbsp Olive oil

2 extra large Eggs

1 tsp Pepper

Directions

Preheat oven to 375 F. Remove mushroom stems and clean out mushroom cups with a damp cloth. Rub olive oil on the outside of the mushrooms. Crack an egg into each cup. Sprinkle with black pepper and any desired herbs to taste. Bake for 20-30 minutes until eggs are set and mushrooms are tender.

Orange

Yields: 1 serving

Ingredients

1 medium Orange

Directions

Peel or slice orange and eat.

Easy Dinner Parmesan Zucchini

Yields: 4 servings

Serving Size: ½ zucchini

Ingredients

2 medium or large Zucchini

2 tsp Olive oil

½ tsp Salt

½ cup Parmesan cheese (grated)

Directions

Preheat the oven to 350 F. Clean the zucchini well, cut the ends off, and slice them lengthwise into quarters so that you have eight pieces. Coat the bottom of a baking dish with the olive oil and place the zucchini pieces in the dish. Sprinkle with the seasoning salt, then with the Parmesan cheese. Place uncovered in the oven and bake for 20 minutes.

Low-Carb Onion Rings

Yields: 12 servings

Ingredients

1 ⅓ cup Vegetable Oil

2 large Eggs

¼ cup Heavy whipping cream (whipped)

2 cups Soy flour

2 tsp Salt

1 tsp Pepper

1 tsp Garlic powder

2 Onions

Directions

Place a heavy pot over medium-high heat with at least an inch of vegetable oil. Heat oil to 350 F (it is important to monitor and maintain the temperature, or the soy flour breading and your oil will burn). In a medium bowl, mix the eggs and cream to make an egg wash. In a separate larger bowl, mix soy flour, salt, pepper, and garlic powder; set aside. Peel and slice the onions in thick slices and carefully separate the rings. Then dip individual onion rings in the breading, then the egg wash, and then back in the breading again, making sure to coat well. Pat off any excess breading and carefully place into hot oil, in batches as necessary, and fry until golden brown and crisp, just 1 to 2 minutes. Remove and drain on paper towels. Serve immediately.

Peanut Butter Chocolate Fat Bombs

Yield: 6 servings

Serving Size: ½ oz

Ingredients

1 stick (8 tbsp) Butter

4 oz Coconut oil

1 tbsp Cocoa powder (unsweetened)

3 tbsp powdered Peanut butter (PB2 or similar)

2 tsp Stevia sweetener

Directions

Place butter into a medium bowl and microwave until melted. Add coconut oil and place bowl back into microwave to melt, if necessary. Add in cocoa powder, peanut butter powder, and stevia; stir until well combined. Once cooled enough to place into a small blender or mix with an immersion blender; place into blender or use immersion blender to thoroughly combine ingredients. You can mix by hand and pour into molds, but the blending helps to ensure all of the ingredients are combined well. Cool in refrigerator or freezer and serve cold.

Low-Carb Crackers

Yields: 6 servings

Ingredients

1¾ cups Mozzarella cheese (shredded)

¾ cup Almond flour

2 tsp Cream cheese

1 medium Egg

Dash of Salt

Directions

Mix the mozzarella cheese and almond flour in a microwaveable bowl. Add the cream cheese. Microwave on high for 1 minute. Stir, then microwave on high for another 30 seconds. Add the egg and salt, and mix gently. Place dough between 2 baking sheets, and roll until thin. Remove the top baking sheet. If the mixture hardens and becomes difficult to work with, pop it back in the microwave for 10-20 seconds to soften again, but not for too long (or you will cook the egg). Cut the dough into small bite-sized pieces. Place each piece on a lined baking tray. Bake at 425 F for 5 minutes on each side, or until browned on both sides and crisp. Cool on a wire rack, and keep in an airtight container in the fridge. If the weather is cool, you may store the container in your pantry for up to 3 days.

Pesto Scrambled Eggs

Yields: 1 serving

Ingredients

3 extra large Eggs

Dash of Salt

Dash of Pepper

1 tbsp Butter

1 tbsp Basil pesto

2 tbsp Sour cream

Crack the eggs into a mixing bowl with a pinch of salt and pepper, and beat them well with a whisk or fork. Pour the eggs into a pan, add butter, and turn the heat on. Keep on low heat while stirring constantly. Do not stop stirring, as the eggs may get dry and lose their creamy texture. Wait until curds begin to form. Add pesto, and mix in well. Cook until eggs have reached desired doneness (but they are still creamy), about 5-7 minutes total. Remove from heat, add sour cream, and mix well. Serve warm.

Zucchetti

Yields: 4 servings

Serving Size: 1 cup

Ingredients

4 medium Zucchini

Salt (to taste)

Directions

Wash zucchini and cut into 2-3" inch chunks. Put zucchini chunks through spiralized, then add to boiling salted water for about 5 minutes. Strain and serve warm.

Creamy Garlic Mushrooms

Yields: 2 servings

Ingredients

½ tsp Olive oil

¼ lb Mushrooms (sliced)

1 clove Garlic (minced)

1 tbsp Whole milk

1 tbsp Cream cheese

½ tsp Basil (ground)

Dash of Salt

Dash of Pepper

Directions

Heat olive oil in a pan over medium heat. Add mushrooms and garlic. Stir and toss until soft and a little liquid is released from the mushrooms. If the mushrooms do not release any liquid, add a couple of tablespoons of milk. Add cream cheese and combine. Add the herbs; season to taste with salt and pepper. Serve straight from the pan, or you can transfer to an oven dish and place in the oven (covered) to keep warm until you are ready to serve. Serve warm.

Low-Carb Maple Pecan Pancakes

Yields: 4 servings

Serving Size: 4 mini-pancakes

Ingredients

1 spray Pam cooking spray

2 large Eggs

⅓ cup Heavy whipping cream

¼ cup Water

1 tsp Vanilla extract

1 oz Splenda (or similar sweetener)

½ cup Soy flour (stirred)

1 tbsp Wheat bran

¼ tsp Baking powder

⅛ cup Pecans (chopped)

Directions

Grease a griddle or large pan with nonstick cooking spray or butter and heat over medium heat. Mix all ingredients except pecans in a blender for about 15 seconds. Stop and scrape down the sides with a spatula, and continue mixing for another 15 seconds until well blended. Pour 16 mini-cakes onto the hot griddle, and sprinkle each with a few pecans. Cook on each side for only a minute or 2. Serve hot.

Superfood Keto Soup

Yields: 4 servings

Ingredients

1 medium head Cauliflower

1 medium Onion

2 cloves Garlic (minced)

¼ tsp Bay leaf (crumbled)

⅝ cup Watercress (chopped)

10 oz Spinach (raw)

4 cups Vegetable broth

1 cup Heavy whipping cream

¼ cup Coconut oil

1 tsp Salt

Dash of Pepper

Directions

Peel and finely dice the onion and garlic. Place in a soup pot or a Dutch oven greased with coconut oil and cook over a medium-high heat until slightly browned. Wash the spinach and watercress and set aside. Cut the cauliflower into small florets and place in the pot with the browned onion. Add crumbled bay leaf. Cook for about 5 minutes and mix frequently. Add the spinach and watercress and cook until wilted (about 2-3 minutes). Pour in the vegetable broth and bring to a boil. Cook until the cauliflower is crisp-tender, then pour in the cream. Season with salt and pepper. Remove from heat and, using a hand blender (or regular blender), pulse until smooth and creamy. Serve immediately or chill and keep refrigerated for up to 5 days.

Baked Parmesan Tomatoes

Yields: 2 servings

Ingredients

6 medium Tomatoes (halved)

⅜ cup Parmesan cheese (grated)

½ tbsp Oregano (dried)

⅜ tsp Salt

2 tbsp Olive oil

Dash of Pepper

Directions

Preheat oven to 450 F. Place tomatoes cut side up on a baking sheet. Top with parmesan, oregano, salt, and pepper. Drizzle with oil. Bake until the tomatoes are tender, about 15 minutes. Serve warm.

Raspberry Greek Yogurt

Yields: 1 serving

Ingredients

6 oz Greek yogurt

10 Raspberries

1 tsp Honey

Directions

In a cup, mix raspberries with nonfat Greek yogurt and honey using a fork. Put in the freezer for 10 minutes if you'd like a "fro-yo" texture, then beat with a fork again. Serve cold.

Sweet Egg Pancake

Yields: 4 servings

Serving Size: 1 pancake

Ingredients

9 large Eggs

8 oz Cream cheese

4 tsp Cinnamon

4 packets Splenda (or other sweetener)

Directions

Warm cream cheese in microwave. Beat in eggs, cinnamon, and Splenda. Pour ¼ of batter into non-stick skillet and cook over medium heat until golden brown on each side. Repeat with remaining batter. Serve hot.

Feta-Stuffed Portobello Mushrooms

Yields: 2 servings

Serving Size: 1 mushroom

Ingredients

2 Portobella mushrooms (whole)

1 cup Feta cheese (crumbled)

1 tsp Salt

½ tsp Pepper

Directions

Clean mushrooms and remove stem and gills with a sharp knife. Dice stems and mix with feta, salt and pepper. Preheat oven to 375 F. Bake mushrooms face down, preferably on a grate or cooling rack placed on top of a baking sheet, for 5-6 minutes. Stuff mushrooms with feta mixture and bake for another 6-8 minutes or until tops of feta turn slightly brown and mushroom has become tender to the touch. Serve warm.

Baby Kale & Blackberry Salad

Yields: 2 servings

Ingredients

4 cups Kale (chopped)

1 cup Blackberries

½ Avocado

4 oz Ricotta cheese

¼ cup Lemon juice

3 tbsp + 1 tsp Olive oil

½ cup Almonds (sliced)

¼ tsp Rosemary (dried)

2 tsp Honey

Salt and pepper, to taste

Directions

Salad: On two large dinner plates, divide and arrange the kale, blackberries, avocado, and ricotta. Set aside.

Dressing: Mix lemon juice, olive oil, salt, and pepper.

Almonds: In a heavy cast-iron pan over medium-high heat, add the olive oil and almonds. Keep the pan moving as the almonds begin to get toasted. As soon as you smell nuttiness, add salt, pepper, and rosemary. Toss for one more second, then add honey. Stir until almonds are coated. Continue for just a few more seconds, remove from the heat, and allow the nuts to cool in the pan for just a few minutes. Add almonds to the salad and drizzle dressing over top.

Low-Carb Blueberry Muffins

Yields: 6 servings

Serving Size: 1 muffin

Ingredients

1 spray Pam cooking spray

2 tbsp Wheat bran

1 cup Soy flour

½ cup Splenda (or other sweetener)

1 tsp Baking powder

2 extra large Eggs

½ cup Heavy whipping cream

2⅔ fl oz Club soda

½ cup Blueberries

Directions

Preheat oven to 375 F. Spray a 6-cup muffin tin with cooking spray. Evenly sprinkle pan with the wheat bran and soy flour mix, being careful to coat the sides of the cups to prevent sticking. Mix all remaining ingredients (except blueberries) with a wire whisk until well-blended. Fold in the blueberries, and fill the 6 muffins cups evenly with batter. Place on the center rack of the oven, and bake for 20 to 25 minutes, or until the tops turn golden brown and a toothpick stuck in the center comes out clean. Remove from oven and let cool before refrigerating. Serve warm with butter or cold with cream cheese.

Chapter 10:

Shopping List

Vegetables
- Spinach (raw)
- Red bell pepper
- Onions
- Garlic (raw)
- Scallions
- Tomatoes (whole)
- Asparagus
- Fennel (raw)
- Jalapeno peppers
- Tomatoes (crushed)
- Canned pumpkin
- Zucchini
- Cauliflower
- Cucumber
- Cabbage
- Ginger root
- Kale
- Watercress
- Portobella mushrooms
- Eggplant
- Broccoli
- Green leaf lettuce
- White mushrooms
- Yellow squash
- Cherry tomatoes

Fruit & Fruit Juices
- Lemon juice (fresh-squeezed, if possible)
- Blueberries (fresh)
- Strawberries (fresh)
- Avocado
- Blackberries (fresh)
- Raspberries (fresh)
- Lemons
- Limes
- Oranges
- Peaches

Frozen
- Strawberries (frozen)
- Blackberries (frozen)

Dairy/Milk

- Cheddar cheese
- Part-skim mozzarella cheese
- Plain Greek yogurt (full-fat)
- Eggs (large or extra-large)
- Butter (unsalted)
- Protein powder
- Heavy whipping cream
- Cream cheese (reduced-fat)
- Parmesan cheese (shredded)
- Ricotta cheese (full-fat)
- Swiss cheese
- Asiago Italian cheese
- Goat cheese (hard type)
- Sour cream (reduced-fat)
- Cottage cheese (large or small curd)
- Feta cheese
- Fontina cheese
- Whole milk
- Egg whites (or separated eggs)
- Romano cheese
- Unsweetened coconut milk (or similar)

Beverages

- Decaffeinated coffee grounds
- Regular coffee grounds
- Club soda

Spices/Herbs

- Black pepper
- Basil (fresh)
- Salt
- Garlic powder
- Basil (dried)
- Cinnamon (ground)
- Lemon zest
- Cumin (ground)
- Onion powder
- Oregano (dried)
- Cayenne pepper
- Pumpkin pie spice
- Thyme (dried)
- Dill (fresh)
- Italian seasoning
- Chili powder
- Bay leaf (crumbled)
- Mustard seed (ground)
- Paprika
- Parsley (dried)
- Peppermint (fresh, whole)
- Rosemary (fresh)
- Garlic salt

Soups/Sauces

- Tomato sauce (no-salt-added)

- Vegetable broth
- Salsa
- Basil pesto

Soy/Legumes
- Soy sauce
- Tofu (silken, firm)
- Soy flour

Nuts and Seeds
- Chia seeds
- Pecans (halved)
- Almond flour (or almond meal)
- Sunflower seed flour
- Canned coconut milk (unsweetened)
- Walnuts (chopped)
- Sesame butter (tahini)
- Almond butter
- Flaxseeds (whole)
- Pumpkin/squash seeds (dried)
- Almonds (whole, raw)
- Powdered peanut butter (PB2 or similar)

Baking Products
- Dried coconut (unsweetened)
- Baking powder
- Baking soda
- Cream of tartar
- Honey
- Splenda (or similar sweetener)
- Dark chocolate cacao nibs (70-85% cacao)
- Semi-sweet chocolate chips
- Cocoa powder (unsweetened)
- Stevia (or similar sweetener)
- Coconut flour
- Agave nectar
- Truvia Baking Blend
- Cocoa butter
- Vanilla extract

Fats/Oils
- Olive oil
- Coconut oil
- Vegetable (canola) oil
- Pam cooking spray (or similar)
- Sesame oil
- Clarified butter (ghee)

Other
- Wheat bran
- Psyllium husk
- Canned olives
- Cider vinegar
- Balsamic vinegar

Chapter 11:

Conclusion

We have finally made it to the final chapter of this cookbook and I'd like to personally congratulate you for making it to the end. We have gone through many concepts, recipes and techniques in the previous chapters that will help you in extracting the total benefits of a vegetarian keto diet. This is not just a diet/lifestyle that sounds good on paper. These recipes, meal plan and the method are very practical and result-oriented. So, if you've gone through the material carefully and are disciplined enough to implement it, you will not be denied positive results. Follow the plan diligently and you are almost guaranteed a definite weight loss of 5kgs within 2 weeks.

But if you feel like you have other travel plans or work load that will become an obstacle in these 2 weeks then you can always schedule a time period later that will support you in your uninterrupted weight loss. Also, if you think you might've missed a few tips or would like more information, don't worry. You can always go back and refer specific sections of this cookbook to quickly find the appropriate fix for your issue.

And last but not least, if you'd like to join a vibrant community of fellow "ketotarians" and other folks that are on the same path as you to live a healthy, happy lifestyle then, make sure to join our group by entering your e-mail list below. You will be added to an exclusive facebook group and receive a Bonus PDF on the Top 3 Secret Tricks to Spike Your Metabolism and Burn Fat Fast. This PDF contains extremely effective insights that will help you take your fitness and physique to the next level. And it has been claimed by some of our previous clients to be the single most valuable resource that gave them quick and clearly visible results. It's a clear win-win for you so go ahead and sign up now at www.bookstuff.in/burn-fat to get the PDF now! Have a great day and hope to see you inside!